UNIVERSITY OF SUSSEX CENTRE FOR CONTINUING EDUCATION

OCCASIONAL PAPERS NUMBER 13

GEORGIAN BRIGHTON 1740 TO 18[illegible]

BY SUE F[illegible]

CW01582645

FIGURES

PREFACE

This is the third and last Occasional Paper based on the work of a tutorial class on 'The History of Brighton 1650-1800' which ran under the auspices of the Centre for Continuing Education from September 1975 to March 1978. Both of its predecessors, Brighton before Dr. Russell (1976) and Aspects of Brighton 1650 to 1800 (1978) were working papers edited by John and Sue Farrant, the joint tutors of the class. This paper attempts to offer a more developed synthesis and takes account of subsequent research by me with assistance from four members of my classes, Mr. Ron Martin, Mrs. Jan Lank, Miss Sue Preece, and, most especially, Miss June Knight who has been working on the material since 1975. The research was helped by Mr. K.T.N. Bryant who lent items from his collection. The British Academy's Small Grants Research Fund for the Humanities gave a grant towards my research. The staffs of East Sussex Record Office, West Sussex Record Office, the Public Record Office, Brighton & Hove Area Libraries, the Keeper of Preston Manor and Rottingdean Grange (Brighton Museum) and Brighton Borough Council (Secretary's Department), have all been very helpful, but the efforts of Mr. Christopher Whittick deserve special thanks. John Farrant, June Knight and John Lowerson commented on the draft of this paper. Mrs. Betty Geeves and Mrs. Jan Lank typed the draft and Heather Payne and June Brinkley at the University the final copy. Steve Frampton of the Humanities Department, Brighton Polytechnic, drew the maps and diagrams. D.R. McPhillips of the University Printing Unit gave much assistance in designing the cover and supervised the printing.

Work is still continuing on the topics and period covered in this paper and on the earlier period. Both John and myself are always pleased to hear from people who have, or know of, documents relevant to this research. Articles which are also based upon the research originally undertaken with the 'Brighton' class are referred to in the references in this pamphlet.

(Dr.) Sue Farrant

Humanities Department,
Brighton Polytechnic,
Falmer,
Brighton. BN1 9PH

November 1980.

Published by the Centre for Continuing Education,
University of Sussex, Brighton, BN1 9RG, 1980.

© Sue Farrant, 1980

ISBN 0 904242 15 3

ISSN 0306-1108

1. THE SETTING FOR CHANGE IN BRIGHTON : THE DEVELOPMENT OF THE GEORGIAN SEASIDE RESORTS TO 1780

Between 1740 and 1770 Brighton was transformed from a decayed seafaring town into a prosperous seaside resort. By 1800 the town was Britain's largest and most fashionable seaside watering place and retained that position into the twentieth century. Brighton's resort development is best appreciated if the origins of this type of town are briefly explored.

Seawater was regarded as a mineral water and its use for health cures arose because of the popularity of drinking and bathing in spa waters. Before the seaside resorts emerged the spa resorts had already developed a standardized social routine and a complementary group of facilities which visitors to both types of watering place, whether seeking a health cure or amusement, soon expected: baths, libraries, assembly rooms, a theatre, a wide range of shops, and lodging houses to rent. By the 1730s, a sojourn in a spa resort was an established part of the annual routine of wealthy people from all sectors of society who were attracted by the integration of the fashion for drinking and bathing in the spa waters with organised leisure activities such as assemblies and cards, supervised by a master of ceremonies. The spa routine provided easily understood regulations of behaviour in addition to planning the visitors' days and helping to integrate an increasingly diverse clientele. Landowners, accustomed to spending part of the year in London or in a provincial capital for access to leisure facilities and town services such as fashionable tailors, and in order to meet their equals, were attracted to spas by their smaller scale, social milieu, and probably by the lower costs of rented accommodation. The concentration of urban leisure facilities and services in spa resorts and the opportunities for social integration provided by the routine were attractive to the increasing numbers of rich townsfolk from the commercial, professional and industrial sectors, who had time and money to spend on leisure. (1)

The success of spa resorts was due not only to the increasingly town-based leisure patterns of the rich, but also to their acceptance of standardized terraced housing based upon simplified concepts of classical architecture. (2) In the late seventeenth century, terraces, crescents and squares such as St. James's Square and Bloomsbury Square were successfully established in London as am alternative to detached town houses for the wealthy. (3) As illustrated by Bath, terraced housing had several advantages for resorts. The homogeneity of facade provided a suitable setting for the resorts' important integrative social role. Terrace design meant that construction was relatively easy, cheap and quick, and the rate of building could be fairly sensitive to fluctuations in demand which was important because any resort needed to catch its visitors' interest quickly once there was a demand for more or better accommodation. Another important asset was that terraces could be built at high densities if suitable sites were expensive, perhaps because of the local topography or a shortage of land for purchase.

Before 1700 doctors recommended sea water drinking and bathing for health cures, but there was little interest until the 1720s and 1730s when seabathing for health and as a leisure activity became fashionable among the middle and upper classes, possibly as a reaction against the formality and the expense of the spas and the exaggerated claims made by doctors for the virtues of spa waters. Due to the wide range of potential sites all round the coast with the ease of access (as compared with a mineral spring which normally required at least a pump within a small building to protect it) seabathing could be an informal and dispersed activity which involved little expenditure by the visitor or the host settlements if there was sufficient accommodation already available. Until the 1750s most references to seabathing suggest that one of its attractions was indeed the informality, but its cheapness was also important. (4)

The earliest reference to seabathing for health is at Whitby in 1718, and someone bathed at Bootle in 1721 for pleasure. In the same year Liverpool was described as convenient for seabathing and a simple bathing hut for undressing was erected there in the 1720s. (5) Further research in correspondence will no doubt reveal more random examples of seabathing before 1730.

In the early 1730s seabathing was easily integrated into the spa routine at the popular resort at Scarborough on the east Yorkshire coast. The spa pump room was at the base of the cliff, a short distance to the south of the town and easily accessible at low tide across a large sandy bay. Dr. Wittie of Scarborough was advocating seabathing as well as using spa waters in the late 1660s, so it is surprising that the earliest reference to seabathing is as late as 1735. (6)

A very important consequence of the established spa resorts' practices was their influence upon seaside resort development. Entrepreneurs who sought to profit from the fashion for seabathing recognised that they could copy most of the spa resort's facilities but that the sea would replace the spa as the focus of activities. Bathing machines and seawater baths were the seaside resort's distinctive novelties, but their acceptance as a major feature of the seaside resort did impose some limitations upon the choice of sites. Bathing machines were apparently developed at Scarborough; one is shown in a print published in 1735, and in a print dated 1744 there is a cluster of machines in the water and on the beach. These cumbersome horse-drawn changing huts were safest upon gently shelving beaches. Baths also needed gentle inclines for seawater to be pumped up to them or, if as at Margate in 1735 and Portsmouth in the 1750s;they were built jutting into the sea, then a sheltered spot was necessary. (7)

From the 1730s seabathing was increasingly widespread (Table 1.1). Some visitors, such as the Rector of Buxted in Sussex, who stayed in Brighton (his nearest costal town) in 1736, had a simple seaside holiday, but increasing numbers sought more formal arrangements. At Margate on the north Kent coast in 1735, an enterprising local carpenter advertised his seawater bath and "convenient lodgings to be lett", which suggests that some people were already aware of the potential of formal seaside resort development. (8)

Because of the expectations of the majority of the clientele, who were already accustomed to the embellishments of the spa resorts and were simply following a fashion, only a few of the seaside places which were frequented for bathing by 1760 emerged during the initial phase of exploration as fully fledged seaside resorts by 1780 (Table 1.1). These new resorts were competing against the spa resorts and had to develop their facilities relatively quickly in order to maintain interest. This in turn confined successful early seaside resort development to towns where both the capital for investment in facilities, and adequate accommodation, were available.

In addition to the success of spas, three more factors particularly influenced the location and timing of the emergence of the first successful seaside resorts. First, catchment: Brighton, Margate and Weymouth, all of which were established as resorts by 1770, benefited from accessibility to large towns and to spas - to Tunbridge Wells and London, to Bristol and Bath - and were located in the prosperous, relatively densely populated south. Scarborough, whose resort role from the 1770s was more dependent upon the sea than on the spa, served the north, particularly the agriculturally prosperous north east with its wealthy towns and gentry. Not until after 1780 when rising

Table 1.1 PLACES RESORTED TO FOR SEABATHING IN BRITAIN c. 1720-1800

Notice how many places were visited, but that the distribution reflects population density - highest in south and southeast England, and possibly the dominance of the middle class visitors from London. The references are mainly to seabathing but some are to resort facilities being built. Many of the places either failed to develop as resorts until in the railway age, or never ever succeeded. For sources, see reference (14).

DATE OF EARLIEST REFERENCE	STRETCH OF COASTLINE			
	South east (London to Isle of Wight)	South west, and Wales	East Coast of England, and Scotland	North west of England
1718-50	Brighton (1736) Margate (1736)	Weymouth (1748)	Whitby (1718) Scarborough (1735)	Bootle (1722) Liverpool
1751-60	Seaford, Eastbourne, Southampton Deal, Littlehampton, Portsmouth, Worthing, Cowes (between 1750 and 1780)		Cullercoats Bridlington Gt. Yarmouth	Blackpool Lytham
1761-70	Ramsgate Herne Bay Whitstable	Teignmouth Tenby	Lowestoft Leith Hartlepool	
1771-80		Lyme Regis		
1781-90	Bognor Folkstone Broadstairs		Cleethorpes Filey	
1791-1800		Sidmouth Barmouth Weston-super-mare	Cromer Skegness W. Mersea Hornsea Withernsea	Southport Rampside

prosperity became more widely diffused socially and spatially could more seaside settlements successfully develop a resort function as a significant part of their economy. (9)

Secondly, access: resorts needed adequate road or water communications with their catchment area. Although Brighton, Margate, Weymouth, and Scarborough, were concerned about access from London as the country's capital city and most important social centre, good links with the respective county capitals, other prosperous towns and spa resorts were important, due to the significant role of the regional clientele in supporting a local resort, particularly during its early years. (10)

Thirdly, the state of the economies of the coastal towns which might become resorts. Brighton, Margate and Weymouth shared several characteristics which contributed significantly to their early success. All three were small coastal towns without vigorous economies which would divert capital and compete for land and labour and so make the establishment of the resort function relatively unimportant. All had suitable beaches and sites, and adequate communications with their catchment areas, due to their function as ports. Their slack economies resulted in surplus accommodation, which provided space for the first flow of visitors, while sufficient capital was available to provide the basic facilities, bathing machines, a library and a rudimentary assembly room. Shops already existed. Trade links with nearby towns gave access to more capital should it be required. Although prosperous coastal towns such as Liverpool, Portsmouth and Southampton attracted seabathing and some speculation in facilities, seabathing failed to compete against their established functions for investment and for suitable sites. (11) The rapid development of the three specialist resort towns also helped to extinguish competition. Even after 1780, when the number of resorts began to increase slowly, small towns or large villages were usually more successful than ventures which involved only one or two people in a small settlement without surplus accommodation and capital, because of the high total cost if all the facilities, including accommodation, had to be built and communications improved. Sir Richard Hotham's unsuccessful development of Hothampton (Bognor Regis) in the 1780s and Jane Austen's Sanditon illustrate the risks. Because expenditure was spread amongst more people in a town, the failure to establish the resort function was not a disaster, conversely, as in Brighton, they could respond rapidly once they chose to invest. (12)

All three pioneer seaside resorts passed through a stage of tentative resort development very quickly and by 1760 had entered upon the second stage of development. Then the resort function dominated the economy and additional land was needed to build housing and services for both the increasing residential and seasonal populations. Brighton rapidly became Britain's major seaside resort, displacing even Scarborough, and its development will be considered in the wider context of the rise of seaside resorts whenever possible, in order to compare similar patterns, and to identify uniqueness and the town's subsequent influence upon other resorts. (13)

2. BRIGHTON: SEAFARING TOWN, 1580 - 1750

The impact of resort development upon Brighton is often over-emphasised by writers who wrongly describe the place as a fishing village which was transformed into a flourishing town because of Dr. Russell's book on the use of seawater (1750) and the visits of the Prince of Wales (1783 onwards). The fact that Brighton was already a town before becoming a resort is important because the scale of the settlement was large enough to influence the location of subsequent resort development. The long period of economic difficulties which

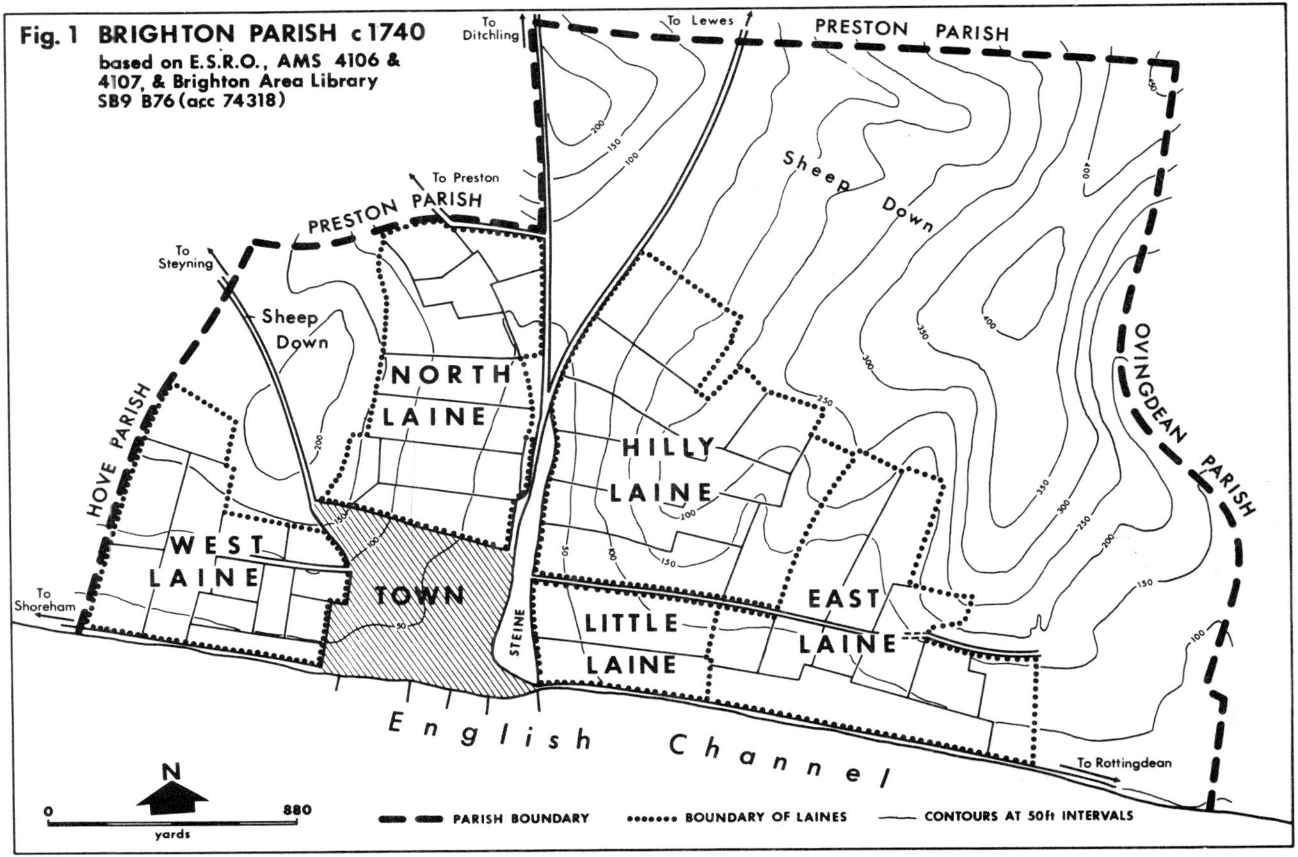

Fig. 1 BRIGHTON PARISH c 1740
based on E.S.R.O., AMS 4106 & 4107, & Brighton Area Library SB9 B76 (acc 74318)

it endured before developing as a resort meant that there was cheap land, an under-employed labour force and townsfolk who were willing to invest in the town's new function in the hope that it would be more profitable than the existing one. The organisation of the land ownership of the farmland which surrounded the town was long established by 1750 and had very significant consequences for the town's physical development when farmland was built on from the 1770s (see Chap. 4).

Even in the 1820s after forty years of rapid development on farmland the town of Brighton was still within the ancient parish boundaries. The ancient parish extended over some 1,600 acres of rolling chalk downland on the dip slope of the South Downs beside the English Channel, where the Downs end sharply as cliffs. The eastern part of the parish is higher than the western end where the downland begins to merge with the low lying coastal plain which extends westwards from the parish boundary (Fig. 1). Two coombes or valleys through the Downs which now carry the London and Lewes Roads, merge about a mile north of the sea to form a single substantial coombe, now known as the Level at its northern end and the Steine further south. The coombe,whose floor and lower slopes are covered by coombe deposits, was once occupied by an intermittent stream fed by springs in Patcham and Falmer parishes to the north of Brighton and which ran down to the Pool where the coombe ended as very low crumbly cliffs. Most of the parish was farmland, and until after 1820 the arable land was organised as five open fields which were subdivided into strips whose owners had the right to pasture sheep on the downland. As time passed both the number of owners of farmland and the number of people employed in farming had declined, but even in the later 1500s farming had not been a major source of employment. The organisation of landownership is discussed in detail elsewhere. (1)

Until the later eighteenth century, the town, where all the parish's inhabitants lived, was bounded by the Steine, the rear of North and West Streets, and the high tide line; the parish church of St. Nicholas lay beyond the town's north-west corner (Fig. 1). The town's site was on the end of a low promontory of downland between the Steine on the east and the coastal plain to the west and part of it is covered by a deposit of coombe rock which overlies the chalk.

In 1650 Brighton had a population of about 4,000 and was the largest town in Sussex, bigger than both Lewes and Chichester, the county towns of East and West Sussex. The basis of the town's prosperity was fishing in the North Sea which was the mainstay of the town's population by the 1540s and sustained population increase until the 1640s. Why Brighton became so successfully involved in the North Sea fisheries is not obvious, but the substantial foreshore below the low cliff on which the town stood was of great significance because it provided an extensive area for workshops, net stores and for beaching the vessels. East of Brighton there were few settlements on the Sussex coast with harbours or good estuarine sites, and of the rest none had a foreshore like Brighton's for the beaching and maintenance of large numbers of fishing vessels.

Within a generation of 1660, the town's fishing was in severe difficulties, some of which afflicted the North Sea fishery generally, such as a slump in demand throughout Europe and enemy attacks on English boats. There was also an important local problem, for by 1650 the erosion of the foreshore was removing the only suitable place for working space and beaching of vessels. By the early 1700s the foreshore had gone and the cliff was being eroded. These problems caused the town to withdraw from the lucrative North Sea fishing, and resulted in the loss of employment.

As fishing contracted from the mid 1650s so coastal trading in which the town was already substantially involved seemed to become more important, although in fact it may not have expanded and failed to sustain the town's prosperity and employment; consequently the population started to fall. The town's dominance of the Sussex coastal trade started to decline in the early eighteenth century and at the same time the average sizes of Brighton vessels and their crews fell. The town's population continued to contract because of the loss of employment to about 2,500 in the early 1740s and about 2,00 in 1750. Brighton's activity in the coastal trade was handicapped by the lack of a harbour and a river link to the town's hinterland. The town's declining economy generated little trade and was a further discouragement to using it as a basis for the coastal trade. Lewes on the River Ouse to the east of Brighton and Shoreham on the Adur to the west had far better access to the region north of Brighton.

Inshore fishing continued but from the late 1600s it did not involve the town's most prosperous seafarers who had previously used their vessels for both inshore and long distance fishing, neither did it employ a large number of men. On observing the activities of inshore fishermen, visitors to the town in the mid 1700s wrongly assumed that it was the major source of employment. The cargo carrying vessels belonging to the town berthed at Shoreham. (2)

Between 1540 and 1650 most of the streets within the old town were established. Certainly the three outer streets (East, North and West) and Middle Street were lined with houses and cottages. The centre of the town around 1600 was an open area, the western part on which Middle Street was already being built, called Hempshares, and the eastern part Bartholomews. On the cliff top, near the blockhouses and the market, stood the Old Ship and the Black Lion Inns, which gave Ship and Black Lion Streets their names. Both streets had a few cottages built along them by the 1650s, mainly near the southern end. By 1650 there were some cottages facing the sea across the market place. A few cottages stood on the southern end of the Steine, on Pool Bank just by Pool Valley, and a cluster of cottages on the Knabb (Brighton Square) was linked by narrow lanes to the bigger streets, such as East Street (Fig. 2). Between 1650 and the 1740s little changed except that the market was moved to Bartholomews because of the erosion of the site on the cliff top. (3)

Brighton in 1744 will be described in some detail to illustrate how simple the little Georgian town was before resort development began, but also to show how the long established layout of the town influenced the development from 1750. This reconstruction is based upon a rate book for 1744, combined with fragments of information from other records such as the manor court books and probate inventories, and describes the town after nearly a century of economic decline and at least fifty years of unemployment that was so severe that the rest of the country had been rated to provide for Brighton's poor (see Chap. 6). (4)

In 1744 there were 453 households in the town, all of which should have paid poor rate but three quarters were exempted because of their own poverty. Only fragments of information have been found about the size, building materials, styles, ages and condition of the houses, but if so many inhabitants were exempt from poor rate due to poverty, then it is probable that their homes were not well kept. Many of the houses were probably very old because townsfolk could not afford to rebuild them. Possibly the buildings were timber-framed, with flint and brick walls and roofs of slate, tile or thatch, some of these building materials being brought by the town's cargo vessels. Bricks may have been made on the west side of the town where, in the early 1720s the honey-coloured bricks for Stanmer House (to the north of Brighton) were produced. Flints from the beach or the farmland were used to build walls for buildings or property boundaries. (5) Because of the town's poverty, even the more fortunate inhabitants had small, simply furnished houses, and few had more than six rooms. Most of their houses had two storeys with an attic and perhaps a cellar or semi-basement. On the ground floor there would have been one main room, sometimes described as a 'hall', but normally as a kitchen

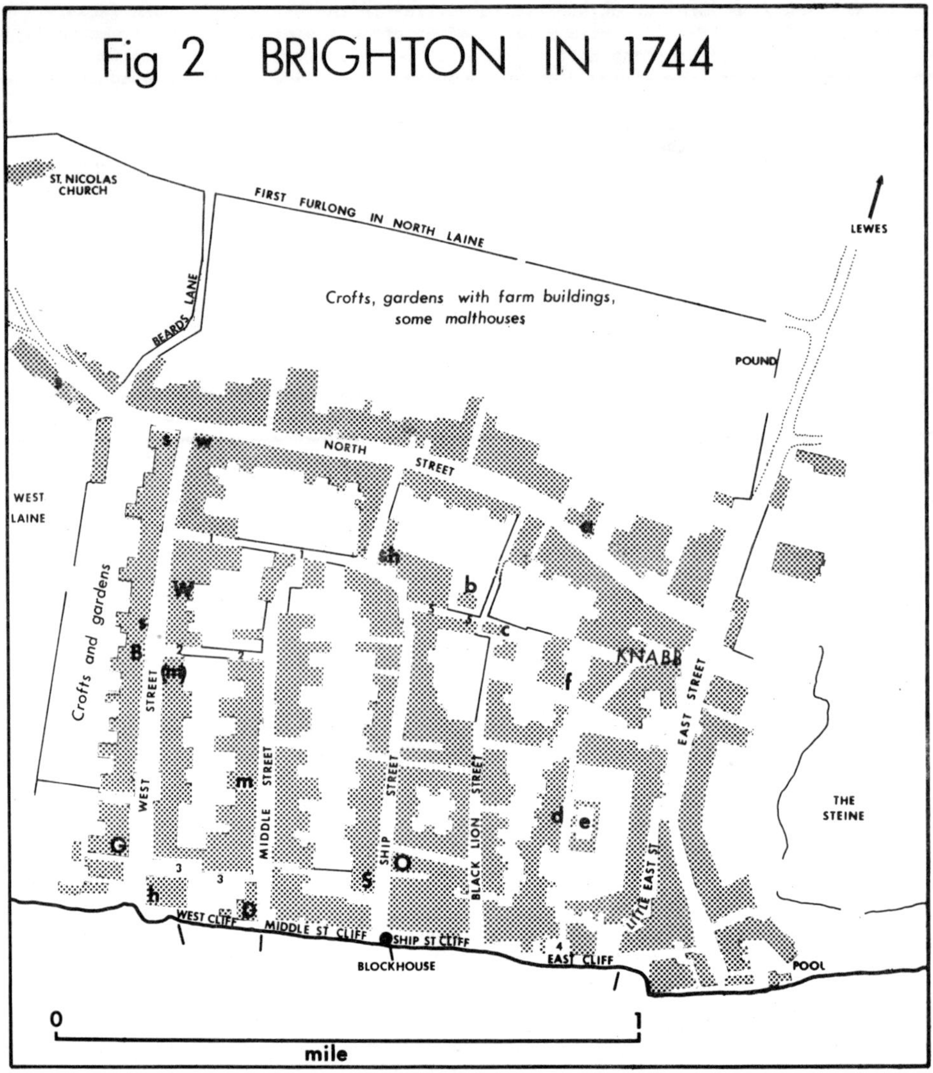

The outline of this map is derived from Fig. 3 and is only intended to indicate where buildings stood.

Key: G George Inn, D Dolphin Inn, S New Ship Inn, O Old Ship Inn, B The Bull. M millhouse (M) probably millhouse. a Quaker's meeting house, b Presbyterian meeting house, c free school, d workhouse and townhall, e market, f vicarage, h herring house, m malthouses, s blacksmith's smithies, sh slaughterhouse, w warehouses, o well. 1 Willetts or Craggs (and later Duke's) lane 2 Boyce's St. 3 South St. 4 Meeting House Lane.

which in many cases contained the only hearth in the house and was entered directly from the street. The other room on the ground floor, if there was one, was called the 'back' or 'inner' room. On the first floor were the two or three bedrooms or 'chambers' which were reached by a narrow staircase, possibly from the kitchen. The garret was in the roof and was normally used for storage. In the yard behind the house there might have been outbuildings, such as a brewhouse or outhouse. If the house was occupied by a craftsman or shopkeeper, then the front part of the groundfloor would be divided into a shop and the kitchen lay behind it. Fragmentary evidence suggests that two rooms in a subdivided house provided a home for many of the poorer people and that some semi-detached and detached houses had only one or two rooms. Dwellings often stood near to or on the street frontage of their plots of land, which were narrowest along the street frontage. In the later eighteenth century the back gardens were often built upon in order to provide more housing and workshops. East Street extended northwards past the end of North Street to the junction with the back Lane which became Church Street (Fig.2) and the town pound was on its north-western corner. This street and its environs, the Knabb, the Steine and Little East Street, were the most densely populated part of the town, and only 19 per cent. of the households paid poor rate. There were clusters of small plots mainly on the street's eastern side, some of which were granted from the manorial waste during the middle and later seventeenth century (possibly as compensation for the loss of holdings by erosion on the foreshore). These small plots were to be an attraction for the first people who developed resort facilities from 1750 (Chap. 3). (6)

Table 2.1 POOR RATE ASSESSMENTS FOR THE TOWN IN 1744

Street	Number of houses: Total	Rate due from	Total rate collected £ p
East Street	58	17 (29%)	19.20
East Cliff & Little East St.	41	4 (10%)	5.40
Knabb	38	5 (13%)	5.40
Steine	12	3 (25%)	8.40
North Street *	84	20 (24%)	26.40
West Street	75	23 (31%)	36.40
Middle Street	60	13 (22%)	22.80
Ship Street	39	26 (87%)	49.80
Black Lion Street	47	6 (13%)	8.40
	453	117 (26%)	182.20

* There were probably more houses than the rate book suggests as some were subsumed under the section headed 'lands' in the rate book. Most of the properties listed as houses stood on the street's south side.

North Street, the town's largest thoroughfare, ran roughly westwards between East and West Streets, then turned northwest to end by the church where it became the road to northwestern Sussex. At this street's eastern end there was a cluster of small properties which became the Castle Inn and Castle Square from the early 1750s. In the later seventeenth century some of the town's master mariners owned properties along the south side of North Street between East Street and a narrow lane now called Poplar Lane, and at least three were lost at sea when their vessels were sunk in a storm in 1703. In 1744 their widows or children still owned the land. Most of the property west of Poplar Lane as far west as West Street was occupied by tradesmen and craftsmen. There was a blacksmith and at least two malthouses (where barley was malted for brewing). In the later 1700s two inns, the Coach & Horses (originally the Lamb) and the Horse & Groom were established along here and probably used the maltings. (7)

Just west of the junction with West Street a track (now Western Road) to West Laine branched off westwards from North Street and on either side of it stood two old established smithies. A large chalkpit on the west side of North Street and opposite St. Nicholas' Church was quarried for limemaking, certainly there are earlier and later references to a limekiln.

The north side of North Street was lined with large crofts which stretched northwards to a back lane (now Church Street) that allowed easy access to them from North Laine. The Quakers Meeting House and burial ground stood on a former croft towards the eastern end of North Street and on its eastern side another croft called Dairy Field eventually became Promenade Grove and then part of the Royal Pavilion estate. Due to the depth of the crofts when development on them eventually started in the late 1770s, streets had to be laid through them along the lines of pre-existing lanes to link North Street with Church Street, in order to build in the central part of the land.

West Street in 1744 had larger houses and crofts on the outermost (western) side of the street and smaller cottages and plots along the innermost (eastern) side. In 1744, some 70 per cent. of the households were exempted from poor rate. The crofts were eventually covered by buildings but the West Street crofts were not as deep as those in North Street and were not developed as streets in the later eighteenth century but as courts and rows which soon declined into slums. In West Street in 1744 there were two inns, a malthouse, a windmill and a herringhouse (for curing herrings) (Fig. 2).

The oldest of the town's three main inner streets was Middle Street, which in 1744 consisted principally of small houses and two inns, one of which had a malthouse and a brewhouse. Three small lanes, South Street, Boyce's and Cragg's (later Duke's), linked West and Middle Streets. The biggest cluster of rate payers lived in Ship Street, where two thirds of the households paid poor rate, by far the highest proportion in the town. Within this very centrally placed street stood the town's largest inns: the Old Ship and the New Ship and a slaughterhouse (Fig. 2), and the town's 'doctor', who was probably an apothecary, lived there. Most of the households in Black Lion Street were exempted from paying poor rate and the only noteworthy buildings were the Black Lion Inn, a malthouse and brewhouse, and a blacksmith's on the street's eastern side near the market. To the west of Black Lion Street stood the small workhouse and town hall. An inventory of the contents of the building was made in 1745 and they included:

> FIRST the Town Clock, having Two half Hundred Iron Weights to it.
> ALSO IN THE HALL......Two pair of Brass Scales and Weights.......

The rest of the building was used as the workhouse and consisted of a kitchen, a workroom with ten spinning wheels in it, a pantry, a brewhouse, two cellars and on the upper floor chambers (bedrooms) with 'eighteen fether bedds with their Appurtenances as they stand'. At the north end of Black Lion Street stood the town's free school and the Presbyterian chapel (Figs. 2, 3). (8)

The town huddled on the cliff top where the blockhouse was crumbling into the sea, in spite of the groynes which had been built in the early 1720s to try to prevent erosion. Surrounding it on its landward sides arable farmland on the down's lower slopes produced cereals, some of which were ground by the five windmills in the parish. One mill stood in West Street, three were in Little Laine, east of the Steine, and the location of the fifth is not known. (9)

Resort development from the 1750s did not obliterate the existing street pattern or the outline of the more distinctive plots of land, such as the crofts in North Street. It changed the appearance of the old town by instigating rebuilding and infilling and the result was that by 1800 the town's landuse was much more varied and there were many distinctive buildings, such as assembly rooms, libraries, chapels and theatres and shops which Brighton had lacked before.

3. THE DEVELOPMENT OF RESORT FACILITIES AND THE SEASON IN BRIGHTON C. 1750 TO 1780

Between 1750 and 1780 Brighton became Britain's largest and most fashionable resort. This chapter briefly discusses why the new function grew so rapidly and concentrates upon the development of the facilities and the attitudes of visitors towards the town as a resort during this important period.

Why Brighton ?

Brighton's resort development is frequently attributed to Dr. Richard Russell, a well-known physician who lived at Lewes, the county town of East Sussex, eight miles north east of Brighton. In 1750 he published a book in Latin called A Dissertation in the Use of Seawater in the Diseases of the Glands. Russell was over 60 years old when he published this book, the first of two on the medicinal use of seawater, a topic in which he had been interested for many years. The Dissertation was published in English in a pirated edition in 1752 and by Russell in 1753, but although the book undoubtedly enhanced his reputation there were already several well-known texts about seawater treatments. His influence on Brighton has been over-rated because the town's important locational advantages have been disregarded and so has the general rise in the popularity of seabathing which Russell so adeptly exploited. (1)

That Brighton, Margate and Weymouth developed as seaside resorts from the early 1750s (Chap. 1) suggests that all three benefitted from sea-bathing becoming increasingly fashionable. This interest resulted in the exploration of the coastline by middle and upper classes in search of places to seabathe as shown in Table 1.1. Brighton was particularly well placed to develop as the first resort on the Sussex coast for serving the regional clientele and, more significantly because of its importance for the town's outstanding success, for attracting Londoners.

Four factors were especially important for Brighton. First, accessibility. Brighton is the nearest settlement on the Channel coast to London and by 1750 the roads between the two towns were adequate though nothing more. Closeness to Lewes, the social centre of the eastern Sussex gentry, and to Tunbridge Wells, the region's fashionable spa, was also of great importance, especially before 1780 because until then many visitors to the town came from the region and visited both Lewes and 'The Wells'. Margate was a rival until the 1770s because it benefitted from cheaper and easier travel to London as visitors came down the River Thames in sailing barges called hoys. But this became a disadvantage to the town's aspirations to be a fashionable resort, because the relatively cheap travel made it too popular with 'unfashionable' Londoners. (2) Margate's problem served to boost Brighton's growth as a fashionable resort, as travel to Brighton was sufficiently expensive and time-consuming to remain a barrier to developing the town as a 'popular resort until the railway was opened in 1841. (3) Secondly, due to the town's economic malaise there was no competition for accommodation, land for development or for labour and so resort development was cheap. Thirdly, access to the beach for people and for bathing machines was easy and around the Steine there was plenty of suitable space for promenading (Fig. 3) Fourthly, prosperous inhabitants of Lewes took a very positive interest in fostering Brighton's growth as a resort; this was particularly important between 1750 and 1780. Some, such as Dr. Russell and Dr. Poole, were actively involved, others lent money as mortgages and bonds and so invested in the town's new function. Wealthy local farmers also lent money. Their role illustrates the importance of regional interest for early resorts and the advantages for a town which was located within a prosperous and socially sophisticated area aware of new fashions through close links with London. (4)

Table 3.1 The Population of the Major Georgian Resorts 1750 to 1821 (5)

Date	Resort							
	BRIGHTON		MARGATE		SCARBOROUGH WITH FALSGRAVE		WEYMOUTH AND MELCOMBE REGIS	
	(A)	(B)	(A)	(B)	(A)	(B)	(A)	(B)
1750	2000(e)		2000(e)		6000(e)		2000(e)	
1761	2000(e)							
1770	3000(e)							
1786	3620							
1794	5669							
1798					7360(e)			
1801	7339		4766		6688		3617	
1811	12012	63%	6126	29%		6%		31%
1818	18000(e)							
1821	24429	103%	7843	28%	8533	20%	6622	40%

KEY (A): population
(B): decadal increase (%)
(e): estimate

From 1750 Brighton's resort facilities developed more rapidly than either Margate's or Weymouth's even though theirs began sooner (Table 3.2). Brighton's progress is particularly striking because of its previous poverty. The town's Georgian resort development can be divided into two phases. In the first, from 1750 to 1780, all of the usual resort facilities were built in the 'old town' (Fig. 3). During the second phase from 1780 to 1820 Brighton's population increased more rapidly than either Margate's or Weymouth's, so that by 1790 both were smaller and in 1821 even Margate's population was less than a third of Brighton's (Table 3.1). The major theme of this phase was rapid growth outwards as lodging houses, residential housing and service buildings were constructed on the farmland and the old town became the business and resort centre for the new suburbs. Between 1811 and 1821 Brighton's expansion reached a peak and the population and the number of houses doubled and Brighton had the fastest growth rate for any town in Britain in that decade.

Table 3.2 Resort facilities in Britain's four major Georgian seaside resorts: comparison of earliest dates of development, 1736-1800. (7)

Facilities	Brighton	Margate	Scarborough (& Falgrave)	Weymouth (& Melcombe Regis)
First record of visitors for seabathing	1736	1736	1735	1748
Doctor's house	1753			
Bathing machines	1754	1753	1735	1769
Seawater baths		1736		1748
Hot & cold baths	1769	1760s	1798	1785
Spa	c.1750		old established	
Assembly room	1752	1750s	1725	1748 (new 1776)
Coffee house	1752		1792	
Library	1759	1766	early 1700s	1785
Theatre	1764, 1773	1761, 1786 plays from 1752	plays from 1730s theatre 1777	1773
MC & organised social life	mid 1760s	1760s	1740s	1778
'Gardens' or walks	1780s		1770s	
Resort accommodation	1750s	1760s	1760s	1770s
Royal family	from 1765			from 1784
Boarding schools	1757			by 1780

The Development of Resort Facilities in Brighton 1750 to 1780

Today a range of statistics can be produced to show the importance of a particular function to a town. For a resort they may include calculations of the number of visitors, their average length of stay, spending patterns, employment generated by them, the number of beds available, and the popularity of some facilities as shown by the number of users. (6) Even today many of these impressive figures are based upon estimates and can easily be challenged but none of the evidence upon which they are based is available for Georgian resorts. The speed and success with which facilities were developed, the impressions and status of visitors, changes in population structure, and the rate of population increase must be used as approximate indicators of the growing importance of the resort function.

The main evidence that Brighton was quick to develop as a resort is the speed at which its facilities were established, for they needed to have a clientele in order to flourish, and by 1780 the town was popular enough to support the full range. The chronology and the location of the facilities will be considered as both aspects are significant. The town's site, layout and existing landuse influenced the location of resort facilities. East Street which became their major centre conveniently linked the easiest access to the foreshore with the junction of the main road from Lewes (and London) and the east-west routeway which passed along North Street (Fig.3). Most of the land to the rear of East Street's eastern side faced both the sea and the Steine, the only sheltered level open ground beside the town, and was owned in small blocks. The south and south-eastern side of East Street offered easy access down a low crumbly cliff to the beach. By 1780 when the full range of specialist buildings had been erected most of them stood on the eastern side of East Street overlooking the Steine.

Development along East Street began in 1752-3 when Dr. Russell built a house for his patients and Samuel Shergold, an innkeeper from Lewes, purchased a large house and converted it into the Castle Inn (Fig. 3). (9) Both buildings stood on the eastern side of East Street where their owners purchased several copyhold tenements for their respective enterprises. The Castle was ideally situated for a coaching inn because it was easily seen as the coaches arrived from Lewes and along the coastal route, and had a good view of the Steine and the sea across the farmland. Russell House on the cliff top was also visible down the Steine and East Street partly because of its large size, but it had the advantage of some shelter by the town from the prevailing winds. The Steine, the valley east of the old town, provided visitors to both places with a sheltered, bare and sometimes very damp promenade. The town was without a safe cliff top promenade until the 1820s.

In 1754 Shergold opened Brighton's first assembly room at the Castle Inn and began to hold assemblies during 'the season' which suggests that Brighton's visitors were already quite numerous. Meanwhile the first bathing machines appeared on the beach below Russell's House. During the late 1750s, a bookseller from Lewes opened a shop in East Street for the season and by 1760 a librarian from Tunbridge Wells had opened a library. (10)

On Russell's death in 1759 there was brisk competition for his practise in Brighton. Dr. Poole of Lewes sought the support of local worthies against the better known Dr. Schoenberg of London (whose portrait, by Lawarence, hangs in the National Gallery) and whose more fashionable reputation resulted in victory. From the 1760s increasing numbers of well-known London doctors visited Brighton for the season in order to treat patients. Several, such as Doctors Lucas Pepys and Anthony Relhan owned houses either on East Street or at the eastern end of North Street close to the fashionable Castle Inn. Dr. Poole was one of the better known local physicians who came to Brighton for the season. In the early 1760s he built a townhouse overlooking the Steine, on the eastern side of East Street. (11)

Two buildings erected beside the Steine illustrate its increasing importance as a promenade, for both were libraries, Jane Austen's novels show how important libraries were as meeting places in resorts. Subscribers signed the visitors' book to record their subscription and to announce their arrival and address to others who might call in to the library to read, chat, listen to music, buy fripperies or gamble. Both libraries are depicted in Lambert's view of 1769 (cover) and on the 1779 map (Fig. 3). Thomas's (later Miss Widgett's) stood near the present Royal York Buildings. Baker's (later Donaldson's) stood on the east side of the Steine (near St. Jame's Street). This library had a little rotunda nearby in which musicians sat and played and was the first resort building to stand outside the town. It remained isolated until the early 1780s when housing was built beside it. Baker's choice of site and his success suggests that visitors found it useful as a place to walk out to across the Steine. Both libraries survived until the 1820s, although more were built in the Steine and Castle Square area after 1800, being attracted by the success of the established one (Table 3.3).(12)

BRIGHTHELMSTON.

Brighton Public Libraries

Bygone Brighton

Map Series - 1

Table 3.3 The Development of Resort Facilities in Georgian Brighton (44)

DECADE	CATEGORY				
	HEALTH	AMUSEMENT	CULTURAL	RELIGIOUS	OTHER
1751-60	Dr. Russell's house Bathing machines Wick Spa ? Dr. Russell's two books Brighton seawater sold in London	Season late June - late September Castle Assembly Rooms	Bookshop, library	Already established: parish church, Quaker's meeting house, Presbyterian Chapel	
1761-70	Awsiter's Baths Wick Spa Pump Room ?	Old Ship Assembly Rooms First visits by members of Royal Family. M.C. appointed	Relhan's <u>History of Brighthelmstone</u> Temporary Theatre in North Street Two libraries on the Steine		First town houses (East St./Steine and east end of North Street)
1771-80		Promenade Gardens c.1780 Castle Assembly Rooms rebuilt	Theatre:North Street	Countess of Huntingdon's Chapel	
1781-90	Mahomed's Baths in East Street	Prince of Wales' first visit and building of Pavilion Horse racing stand	Theatre:Duke Street (replaced above)		S. end of Steine landscaped Suburban development on fields successfully started
1791-1800				Chapel Royal in North Street	S. Steine by Castle levelled and drained
1801-10	Royal Baths, Pool Valley	New M.C. Season late July - late Dec.	Brighton Herald newspaper Theatre: New Road (replaced above)	Church St. Chapel, St. James's St. Chapel, Dorset Place Chapel	
1811-20	Artillery Baths	Season late July - March Pavilion remodelled	Regular promenade concerts. Eight new libraries, mostly near the Steine. Botanic Gardens. Picture Gallery.	Ship St. Chapel, Cumberland St. Unitarian Chapel	Enclosure of N. Steine

Brighton's first baths were built in 1769 in an area which attracted competition later (Table 3.3). Dr. Awsiter built his hot and cold seawater baths at the south-eastern end of East Street (Fig. 4) where the cliff on which the old town stands slopes down into the mouth of the Pool and where pipes could most easily be laid to pump seawater up to the baths. The site was also close to the most popular area for seabathing and the bathing machines until 1800 when segregated bathing beaches were arranged. (13)

The increasing number of visitors attracted John Hicks of the Old Ship in Ship Street (Fig. 4) to invest in resort facilities and in the 1760s he built assembly rooms, the first opened in 1761. (14) During the 1760s the town had a makeshift theatre in a barn on the north-west corner of Castle Square. In 1764 when it was used by the Chichester Company of Players there was a stage, two galleries and a pit. (15) Other ventures which began in this decade were the Countess of Huntingdon's Chapel in North Street which opened in 1761 and had to be enlarged in 1769 (Fig. 3), and private boarding schools. (16) By 1761 a chalybeate spring at Wick in Hove was used by those for whom doctors recommended more traditional treatment or who simply preferred it, and a pump room was probably built over it in the 1760s.

The only important facility that was missing in 1770 was a proper theatre and once it was opened in North Street in 1773 the town had everything that the visitor would expect (Fig. 3 and Chap. 4). (17) From 1780 the process of development of buildings consisted of improving and enlarging existing premises and building more of some facilities such as baths and libraries as the number of visitors increased (Table 3.3). Even in 1821 most of the development was in the East Street - Castle Street - Steine area, by which date the town's extensive eastern suburbs made it very central for visitors (Fig. 7). In 1770 Brighton was not yet unique for Margate's resort facilities had also developed, but from then the duplication of facilities in the Sussex resort reflected a speed of development which Margate failed to achieve and Brighton became Britain's major seaside resort (Table 3.2). (18)

A season during which fashionable visitors came soon developed at Brighton, normally beginning in late June and during which a daily routine was focused upon the increasing variety of resort facilities. Until a master of ceremonies was appointed in the later 1760s the town's leading innkeepers organised the season's activities, which were very simple at first. (19) In the 1750s when he owned the town's only assembly rooms, Samuel Shergold of the Castle Inn formally advertised the start of 'the season' which really meant that he was holding assemblies twice a week in the evening. Visitors had to fill the day themselves. People rose early, at about 6 a.m., to sea bathe because doctors recommended it and then breakfasted afterwards. Visits to the bookshop, further exercise, or watching sports such as cockfighting, filled the day. After dinner a visit to the assembly rooms for a ball or on other nights for cards, visitng friends, reading, music or playing cards filled the evening. (20)

When the rooms at the Old Ship were opened in the early 1760s and both places had coffee houses the evenings were more fully occupied. Both innkeepers used their improved rooms more and organised public teas during the afternoon. As the number of visitors and range of activities increased in the 1760s, so the appointment of a master of ceremonies became necessary for he could co-ordinate the resort's activities and integrate different groups of visitors most of whom shared a similar social status and interests, and many of whom were familiar with the spa resorts of Tunbridge and Bath. (21)

Captain Wade was the town's first master of ceremonies and was active from the late 1760s until 1808. No detailed description of any aspect of the resort routine before 1800 has been found and the following description of its development with an M.C. officiating to 1780 is based upon a variety of sources. The organisation of the Georgian resort routine presumed that visitors should live publicly and so new arrivals were expected to subscribe to several places where they would meet, such as the assembly rooms, a library, baths, and the charges were published by the master of ceremonies in consultation with the respective owners. A copy of the earliest list of charges found, for 1800 is reproduced as Table 3.4.

These subscriptions were quite an expensive aspect of resort life which helped to limit the number of visitors. Another was paying for accommodation for a stay which could last several weeks. Most visitors arranged to rent furnished lodging houses in advance and sent some of their own servants to settle in before they arrived. Even in 1800 only a few visitors owned their own residences, for most did not return every year. If suitable accommodation had not been arranged in advance then an inn would be used until terms had been agreed for a house. Single men normally remained at inns or used one of the few boarding houses.(22)

Having settled into their accommodation the visitors were soon integrated into the daily pattern if they chose to join in. The day began with sea-bathing or a visit to the baths between 6 and 9 a.m. The bathing machines lacked awnings and bathing was a mixed, public affair until the sexes segregated in 1800. After bathing and paying the pair of bathing women or men who attended each machine and the boy (if one was employed to manage the horse which pulled the machine in and out of the water), then the bathers returned to their lodgings or went to the coffee rooms in the two big inns or (from about 1770) to one of the coffee houses to read the papers, talk or write letters, and to breakfast unless they were going to a public breakfast. These were arranged in both the Old Ship and the Castle from the early 1770s. From the early 1780s they were also held in the Promenade Gardens (now New Road), enlivened by concerts, dancing and fireworks until the gardens were sold to the Prince of Wales in 1802 to enlarge the Pavilion's grounds.(23)

After breakfast some people went to church or to chapel choosing in the later 1760s between the parish church, the Countess of Huntingdon's Chapel, the Quaker's Meeting House in North Street, and the Presbyterian Chapel near Ship Street. In 1793 the Chapel Royal in North Street was opened but no more religious edifices were built until 1808 (Table 3.3) though some of the existing ones were enlarged before then.

The afternoon was filled with diverse amusements: promenading, riding on the Downs, watching cricket matches and other entertainments on the Steine, visiting shops, reading or chatting in the libraries and bookshops and attending public teas. In the evening the M.C.'s arrangements were particularly important because he integrated an increasing number of entertainments into a pattern which gave variety and reduced competition between the main highlights such as the dress balls and theatre evenings.(24) By 1780 the daily resort routine was established and remained unchanged until the 1820s.

Visitors were also diverted by a variety of other activities some of which could absorb the whole day. The springy short turf of the downlands surrounding Brighton is good for horse riding and racing and the local gentry had established annual races near Lewes by 1718. Visitors to Brighton went to Lewes races which was a major social event for the area. From 1783, races

Table 3.4 Subscriptions for resort facilities in 1800

Source: Cobby

iv. INTRODUCTION.

The Terms of Admission to the Balls, Assemblies, and to Tea and Promenade, are as follows :— A Gentleman's Subscription for the Season, 10s. 6d.—A Lady's Subscription for the Season, 10s. 6d.— For each Ball, 3s.—Tea and Promenade, 1s.—Non-Subscribers for each Ball, 5s.—Sunday Tea and Promenade, 2s.—Card Assembly Nights, 1s.

The THEATRE, in Duke-street, opens early in JULY, and closes about the End of SEPTEMBER. The Days of performing are Tuesdays, Wednesdays, Fridays, and Saturdays. The Doors open at Six o'Clock, and the Performance begins at Seven o'Clock. Boxes, 4s.—Pit, 2s.—Gallery, 1s.

The BATHS.—They were built in the Year 1768, from a Plan of Doctor Awsiter's; they consist of two Cold Baths,—four Hot Baths, and a Showering Bath.

The Subscription to the Hot Bath is, for Three Months, £10 10s.—Two Months, £7 7s.—One Month, £4 4s.

The Subscription to the Cold Bath is, for Three Months, £3 3s.—One Month, £1 11s. 6d.

Non-Subscribers pay for Cold-Bathing, 1s. 6d., and for Hot-Bathing, 4s.

Subscriptions are not admitted for the Showering Bath—each Person pays for the use of it, 1s. 6d each Time.

If any Bath be wanted at any particular Hour, Notice for it may be given at the Bath House, where Persons are always in waiting.

The SEA-BATHING from the Machines, both at the East and West End of the Town, is particularly safe and pleasant—the Expence is, 1s.

At Wick, which is distant little more than Half a Mile Westward from the Town of Brighthelmston, there is a Spring of Chalybeate Water, which has been found particularly serviceable in most Cases of Debility and Indigestion, and in other Cases, where tonic remedies are required. There is a small Building over it, where Attendance is constantly given from the beginning of May till November, from Nine in the Morning till Six o'Clock in the Evening.

Subscriptions for the Season, 10s. 6d.—Non-Subscribers per Glass, 6d.—Non-Subscribers per Bottle, 6d.

Besides the Public Assembly Rooms and Theatre, there are also in Brighthelmston, PUBLIC GARDENS, that open at the beginning of JUNE, and close about the End of OCTOBER.

Terms of Admission :—Family Subscriptions, 10s. 6d. — Single Subscription, 5s. 6d.—Non-Subscribers, 6d. each.

The BRIGHTHELMSTON RACES, perhaps the best in England, with the Exception of Newmarket and York, are fixed by the Steward, Sir Thomas Charles Bunbury, Bart., with Lord Egremont, and other the principal Nobility of the County, at the close of JULY or the Commencement of AUGUST.

The RACE STAND, which completely commands the Course, and a most excellent View of Beachy-Head, and the intermediate Sea and Country, was built by Subscription in 1788. It stands 385 feet above the Level of the Sea at low Water, and the distance you command from it on the Sea, is nearly 25 miles. The Admission to the Stand, or to the Betting Ground, is 2s. 6d. each Race Day.

PLEASURE BOATS.—These (with Attendants) may be had at Wallis's, at the Rising Sun, in East-street, at One Guinea each per Day ; or Half-a-Guinea for a short Excursion.

Source: Cobby.

were also held on the site of the modern Brighton race course for three days in late July or early August when the season was in full swing. When notables such as the Duke of Cumberland and the Prince of Wales attended, so did other visitors without local connections, otherwise the spectators were mostly local gentry who were normally the owners of the horses. At first the events were organised from the Castle Inn but from 1788, when the first race stand was built, local enthusiasts became responsible. The first stand had an unfortunate history, the roof lead was stolen at least once and in 1803 the structure was destroyed by fire and replaced. The M.C. called the formal assemblies in race week the Race Balls.(25)

Novelty races were popular entertainments, and in the 1750s and '60s visitors travelled over the downs to Rottingdean to the east of Brighton to watch racing,for prize money by men and,for articles of clothing by women. Cricket matches there also attracted spectators and were played for prize money. By the early 1770s the same type of races were being held on the Steine and jackass races were also arranged there. Cricket matches at Rottingdean were supplanted at about the same time by games on the Steine where the teams became increasingly respectable as prosperous townsfolk teamed up with visitors to play. Yet again gambling was involved and the teams played for prize money.(26)

By the late 1780s the Steine was being used for a variety of activities including informal ball games as well as the spectator sports described above. It was decided that part of the land should be palisaded and turfed and kept for the decorous promenaders and all other activities were forbidden in this area. The M.C. announced that people who chose to ignore the arrangement could be fined. Entertainments were pushed north of the Pavilion (Fig. 6) until 1818 when this area was also enclosed and then the Level was left as the last large recreational area.(27)

Many visitors must have occupied themselves with activities which they organised themselves or discovered by inquiry, such as local hunts, obtaining game licences in order to shoot, going out for rides to local scenic spots such as Stanmer Park and the surrounding villages. From 1810 local guide books helped them to select their routes by enthusing about places which suited the fashion for the picturesque such as Preston Manor and the nearby woodland called the Rookery.(28) They could watch bloodsports which included bearbaiting and cockfighting arranged in the yards of the smaller inns and in the surrounding villages. Boxing matches were organised in the same places. (29) The sea was also used for entertainments such as yacht races and water parties which were watched from the shelter of the Steine. Military manoeuvres on the Steine and the Downs were popular.(30)

The rapid development of a full range of resort facilities and the lengthening of the formal season during which they were all open reflected the town's success. In the 1760s the formal season began in late June and lasted only until the end of September but the M.C. organised a few formal assemblies up to the first week or so of December. By 1804 the season started in late July but lasted until after Christmas and by 1818 until March.(31) The season was increasingly a fashionable event, and for the rest of the year the town was occupied by invalids and others who came to enjoy the sea while accommodation was cheaper and quieter.

How many people came for the season and who were they? Although numbers undoubtedly increased and the length of visits probably did, there is little evidence of the actual numbers. There are a few estimates but these cannot be relied upon as can be seen in Table 3.5.

Table 3.5 Estimates of the number of visitors and the resident population (32)

Year	Visitors			Resident population
1769	Minimum		320	3,000
1787	July-Oct. library list		2,000	3,800
1794			10,000	5,700
1811			12 or 15,000	12,000
1817-18	June-Oct.	7,000)		
	Nov.-Feb.	2,300)	11,000	18,000
	Feb.-June	1,700)		

The upward trend was interrupted by the effects of national economic slumps (which also slowed down building in Brighton, as discussed in Chap. 4). Original Visitors' Lists or Subscription Lists from the libraries have not survived. The earliest compiled list is dated 1769 and is arranged in alphabetical order which suggests that it was culled from a library list at the end of the season. There are 320 visitors of whom about one in eight had titles. Some of the visitors without knighthoods or peerages were obviously related to those who did have them. Because there are no addresses and few initials, further analysis is difficult. Some of the nobility and gentry held land in Sussex, such as the Abergavennys of Erredge, the Egremonts of Petworth, Sir Ferdinand Poole, members of the Sussex branch of the Pelham family, and Lord Bridger. Perhaps Captain Lechmere was related to the Worcestershire family of Hanley Castle and the 'Mr, Mrs and 3 Misses Foley' came from the same county but what can be made of 'Captain Cook' and 'Mr. Brummell'?(33) From the late 1780s the county newspaper published visitors lists compiled from the libraries' subscription books during the early part of the season but with even less detail than the 1769 list described above.

Special visitors such as members of the Royal Family and the Russian ambassador were always noted in the newspaper. The first notables were both members of the Royal Family, the Duke of Gloucester in 1765, and then the Duke of York in 1766. From 1771 the Duke and Duchess of Cumberland were regular visitors and the town's popularity with his uncles might have been one reason why the Prince of Wales came in 1783 when he stayed for eleven days.(34)

Visitors' impressions of the resort as it developed to 1780 are important because their reactions influenced its success. But diaries and letters are difficult sources to use as evidence for the reasons for the author's description cannot be established. In spite of some of the comments below the majority of the visitors must have liked Brighton as it became increasingly popular. Favourable comments by acquaintances must have been as important to people who visited resorts for their novelty and so for recreation, as the recommendations of physicians. Publicists' descriptions of the town can be compared with visitors' remarks. Dr. Relhan claimed in 1761 in his History:

> 'the town improves daily as the inhabitants, encouraged by the late great resort of company, seem disposed to expend the whole of what they acquire in the erecting of new buildings or making the old ones convenient. Should the increase of these (improvements) in the next 7 years, be equal to what has been in the past (7 years) it is

probable that there will be but few towns in England that will exceed this in commodious buildings.'(35)

One visitor in 1766, gave the most succinct summary of why people visited and his remarks are supported by most of the contemporary descriptions which have been found so far:

> 'Brighton is a small ill-built town, situated on the sea coast, at present greatly resorted to in the summer season, by various persons labouring under various diseases, for benefit of seabathing and drinking seawater ... and by the gay and polite on account of the company which frequent it in this season ....'(36)

Some of the visitors to Brighton were ordinary local people such as Thomas Turner, a shopkeeper of East Hoathly, who was not impressed by the place, as in 1757 he persuaded his brother to bathe at Seaford instead of Brighton in case he got into 'bad company'.(37) The pair walked to Seaford from East Hoathly and back in the day.

Some visitors believed in the seabathing and enjoyed the company and described both. In 1763, one newcomer found that seabathing agreed with him, liked the novelty and remarked:

> 'It would astound you to see the mixture of sexes at this place, and with what coolness and indifference half a dozen Irishmen will bathe close to those whom we call prudes elsewhere ....'(38)

(Bathers still bathed naked.) But in the same year another visitor claimed: 'I think all public places are alike for it is just like Bath and you see a vast many fine folks ....'(39) Not all visitors liked their fellow company, one diariest described the people who went to the assemblies and to the coffee rooms at the Castle as 'vicious and fashionable' and 'uncivil'.(40)

By the early 1770s there is less sense of novelty and the routine of an established resort is reflected in contemporary descriptions. In 1771 John Baker

> 'took lodgings instantly at Miss Grover in West Street at 1 guinea a week man and self. Met Mrs. Charles Ashburnham, Mr. Baysford and others. Subscribed to the coffee house, five shillings to the rooms, three shillings to the circulating library.'

He seabathed early the next day and while in Brighton went to the races at Lewes.(41)

By the late 1770s detractors no longer described the resort as primitive but instead accused it of exploiting visitors or ostracised the latter for their social origins and behaviour. Other resorts, including Bath generated similar comments; perhaps Smollett's Humphrey Clinker is one of the best literary examples. In 1780 one author deemed Brighton

> 'Only an obscure fishing village .... until silken folly and bloated disease under the auspices of Doctor Russell deemed it necessary to crowd the shore and fill the inhabitants with contempt for their visitors.'(42)

These visitors came for seabathing and its associated amusements and thought of the town as a seaside spa. The town prospered and became fashionable because of their interest and this attracted the Prince of Wales who visited in 1783 just as the town's second phase of development began and the suburbs started to envelop the 'old town'.(43)

4. THE BUILDING OF A SEASIDE RESORT, BRIGHTON 1750-1820

Between 1750 and 1820 Brighton's extent and appearance were dramatically changed. The old town was virtually rebuilt and surrounded on all of its landward sides by suburbs built upon the farmland. (Compare Figs. 3 and 4.) The increase in population and prosperity created a demand for the obvious resort facilities such as baths, libraries and accommodation and for the ordinary but essential requirements of any growing town: houses for its residents, workshops, shops, mews for horses.

At first all urban developemnt was within the old town (Fig. 3) but from 1780, after thirty years of infilling and rebuilding, shortage of space and the town's increasing popularity combined to encourage suburban development on the fields where the first successful projects were rows of lodging houses just east of the Steine (Fig. 4). Suburban development changed the role of the 'old town' which became a town centre.

Change in the 'old town' 1750-1820

By 1760 the old town's eastern side was established as the area where resort development would be concentrated, because of the importance of the Steine as an open space and the availability of suitable sites for building the main resort facilities between East Street and the Steine, as described in Chapter 3. Although the southern end of East Street was the first area to be directly affected by the town's emergence as a resort, by 1780 Castle Square at the junction of East and North Streets was becoming a busy thoroughfare and shopping centre, and from 1780 shops spread westwards up North Street as the old town became a town centre within the suburbs. The presence of the Pavilion at the northern end of East Street from the mid 1780s helped to deflect both resort and ordinary town development westwards by preventing development north of Castle Square and further enhancing the growth of North Street as the town's main shopping street. The Promenade Gardens which flourished on the western side of the Pavilion from the early 1780s to 1800, the enlargement of the Pavilion and its grounds from the late 1780s, the opening of the Theatre Royal in New Road in 1808 all helped to sustain the status of North Street and Castle Square into the 1820s and kept the resort facilities within the East Street - North Street axis.(1)

Although East Street was the first area to be directly affected by resort development in the early 1750s, by 1760 there is evidence of some re-development in most of the streets. Investment in Brighton as a resort can conveniently be divided into two types. The first is in the provision of specialist leisure facilities. Most of these cost more money to develop and needed a more specialist knowledge of the resort clientele's needs in order to make them successful than the second type, the building of houses, shops and workshops. In the old town both types of investment were important because they changed its appearance.

From the 1750s and 1760s assembly rooms and theatres were built in many provincial towns which were larger than Brighton. But in Brighton the rate at which leisure facilities were built between 1750 and 1780 is particularly striking because of the town's small size and the lack of a wealthy resident population until the 1770s. Assembly rooms cost between £2,000 and £5,000 to build in the 1750s and 1760s: the Bristol assembly rooms were built in 1754-5 (just after Shergold built his rooms at the Castle Inn in Brighton) and cost £3,500 for a coffee room, a tavern and a lobby on the ground floor with the Assembly Room on the first floor. The layout is similar to the Castle Inn's first rooms, although the sizes of the respective buildings are not known.(2) When rebuilding the assembly rooms in the late 1770s and subsequently refurbishing them, Shergold borrowed money by raising mortgages on the inn and by entering into partnership. As the mortgagees in the 1770s were Lewes businessmen and local gentry, Shergold probably raised the money to build the first assembly rooms in the same way. John Hicks at the Old Ship mortgaged his inn to local gentry to raise some of the cost of his assembly rooms in the early 1760s. Both owned their own inns and could plough back profits into improvements and use the inns as security for loans. Dr. Awsiter, the wealthy physician who built the first small baths, probably purchased the land and paid for the building without borrowing money because the baths were so simple in design.

The most speculative leisure venture was the town's theatre because of the problems of getting an enterprising manager or owner-manager who could attract good players and choose the right programmes to fill the house at most performances. Theatres in resorts were open for short seasons and had to make enough money to pay the employees, keep the equipment and costumes in good order, and give a profit to the owner. The buildings were usually simple in exterior design, and it was the interiors that were expensive because of the need to provide seating and all the props. Brighton's first theatre was built in 1772-3 by Samuel Paine, a builder, on his own land in North Street (Fig. 3). Paine was the only Brightonian who was a major investor in a resort facility, all the others being incomers who borrowed money from investors who also lived elsewhere. Paine must have had advice on theatre construction from a theatre manager. Indeed the idea of a theatre may have been suggested by a prospective manager such as his first one, Mr. Johnson. As the land owner and a builder by trade, Paine was probably able to build quite cheaply, but even without the cost of purchasing land theatres cost around £1,000 to build.(3) In the early 1780s Mr. Fox who managed the theatre at Lewes took over from Mr. Johnson and managed both. The North Street theatre was supplanted in 1790 by a new one in Duke Street which was built by a timber merchant, Stephen Poune (who owned the land), in partnership with an auctioneer called Henry Stiles. This larger and more lavish theatre was described in July 1790 as 'little inferior to the Haymarket'.(4) The Duke Street theatre forced the one in North Street to close but its interior was unfinished in 1792 when Fox died and it had cost at least £2,500 by then. Not until 1796 was the interior properly decorated which suggests shortage of money. In 1807 it was closed and demolished because of the opening of the bigger, more lavish Theatre Royal in New Road which again proved to be an expensive (and probably unprofitable) undertaking for its investors. The building cost is estimated at £6,000.(5) Nevertheless, most resort facilities were profitable for their owners and secure investments for the mortgagees because of the town's increasing success as a resort, but their success also depended on adequate management, which the majority had in Brighton.

The second type of investment was in the general improvement of the town's buildings, in redevelopment and infilling. Although less ostentatious than the type described above it was very important and transformed the town's appearance because of its extensiveness. It also committed many people to Brighton's future as a resort because they invested their own money and borrowed other people's money in order to benefit from the town's increasing prosperity.

Many families became involved in changing Brighton as people could become investors in a variety of ways. Although most of the land in the town was copyhold and not freehold the type of tenure did not deter development, for copyholders could sell all or part of their land as they wished and paid only nominal dues to the lord of the particular manor from which they held it. Most land owners in the town could not afford to build new houses or extend existing properties in order to let rooms or add workspace, without borrowing money on mortgage or selling some land to raise the money to build on the rest. The sale of land gave immigrants and local people who could afford to buy, the chance to do so and they would either buy outright or pay a deposit and raise a mortgage for the balance. The new landowners then sought investors to lend them money so that they could build on their land using it as security for the mortgage. Thus two groups of people with land sought for people to lend money. As the town's inhabitants did not have enough capital they sought loans from people in the surrounding region and between 1750 and 1780 many people from Lewes and the area of Sussex between the Adur and the Cuckmere lent money to Brighton's townsfolk. Gentry, craftsmen, retailers, professional people and farmers all lent money, and Brighton became a magnet for local investors. From the 1780s the town's net spread more widely and middle class Londoners became an important source for investment.(6)

The town's 'developers' were its tradesmen and women who owned the shops, workshops, inns, and coaching businesses, and the professional people and their families. Builders were also important developers because they could buy, develop and sell small plots while being employed by small business people to build on their own land. Brighton's revival and redevelopment was typical of the thriving Georgian town, large or small. Many of the properties were built for letting, not only to visitors but for other businesses and for residence. Although a large proportion of the housing was indeed built for seasonal letting, either as apartments with the owner providing cooking and cleaning, or as an entire house, not all of it was suitable either because the site was not well positioned or because the plot was too small. A lot of cheaper housing was needed for the servants and other employees and less affluent tradesmen, and the provision of such housing was profitable and less speculative than 'resort' accommodation which was a competitive and less stable market.(7)

The size and location of plots had important consequences for their development. Land on the main streets was always more valuable than land within the street blocks and often deep plots were subdivided in order that the valuable street frontage could be exploited by selling it off for lodging houses or for a house with a shop or with these newly built on it, but with provision for access to the residual land behind which could be used for cheaper housing, workshops or mews. All of the land around East Street, and within the area bounded by East Street, the south side of North Street and the east side of West Street was conveniently developed by subdivision as described above. The crofts in North and West Streets which are discussed in Chapter 3, and are shown on Figs. 3 and 4 needed a different approach. Here the problem was that the depth of the land made access to the street difficult to arrange if the land was divided into the small house plots which most people wanted.

In North Street paths through the crofts became streets and the land on either side was divided into building plots and sold off in a piecemeal fashion. The first buildings on the crofts were small lodging houses which were intended for sale or for leasing. But competition from the new lodging houses built on the cliff top to the east of the town from the early 1780s, and the rise of North Street as the town's major thoroughfare changed the character of the streets which were quickly occupied by tradesmen. In West Street, where most of the crofts were smaller than those in North Street, the owners either slowly invested in developing them or sold them to developers who laid them out as courts of small cottages,provided access from West Street via an alleyway; and either sold off the plots for building or, more frequently, developed them and sold the properties. This area was on the town's western fringe when it was built over and the land was cheap, due to its isolation from resort development on the town's eastern side and its failure to attract better class development facing westwards to the sea.(8)

Although the process of development was continuous it increased in rate from the 1750s. By 1820 it had reached the stage where properties built in the earlier years of the resort were being demolished for redevelopment. Between 1750 and 1820 phases of development can be detected. In the first phase between 1750 and 1770 many of the buildings were being built in a vernacular style, using mainly flint with brick facings. Most of the houses were probably of two storeys with a garret, and built lengthwise along the street. Even large houses such as the original 'Marlborough House' built by Shergold in 1769, facing the Steine (replaced by the present house in c.1787) were built in the same way because land was cheap. From about 1770 the second phase began when land values along main streets and the cliff top increased. Houses in fashionable areas became taller and narrower: this was especially noticeable in East and North Streets where bow windows were introduced to light the narrow rooms. As the main street frontages were infilled, from the mid 1770s,building along the smaller streets such as Duke Street and Boyces Lane became more densely packed, Market Street began to link Little Castle Square on the cliff to Brighton Place (Fig. 4) and the crofts in North and West Streets were built on. By 1780 more space for lodging houses was urgently needed and that resulted in the beginning of suburban development.

The final phase in the old town's development was between the mid 1780s and 1820 when it became very densely built up but more specialist in function, because the new suburbs provided resort accommodation. The old town became the service centre, like a modern town centre today, with shops, professional services and inns. The inns provided accommodation for visitors who sought lodgings or who were in the town on business: many people came to sell goods, invest money or discuss personal affairs with their clients who were staying in the town. Inns also provided food, horses and carriages, and were calling places for postmen, carriers and stage coaches and so needed to be centrally located.(9)

By 1820 the fashionable main streets hid densely packed artisan housing and slums. In North Street, Mulberry Square, the area near Air Street, and the inner area of the block of land on the eastern side of the junction with West Street were rookeries. Properties to the rear of the west side of West Street had also deteriorated to a similar level, particularly between Half Moon Court and the seafront. Perhaps the most notorious area was Kent's Court, built by the Kent family (who were builders) from the late 1770s. All these areas are described in detail in Health Reports written in the 1840s. (10) The old town began to deteriorate as it became hemmed in by the suburbs, all of which started to develop their own shopping areas by 1820. Only North Street retained its aura of prosperity and this was because this street was so accessible from all the town's suburbs and had the main coaching and carrier services operating from inns and coach offices along it. The tightly built up old town, with its medley of building styles and wide range of buildings of 1820, was mainly post 1750 in date yet it seemed 'old' in 1820 when compared with the large area of buildings which were built around it on the fields, mostly since 1800.

Building on the farmland 1780-1820

From the 1780s a series of suburbs spread out at different speeds over the surrounding arable land. By 1800 the suburbs housed a substantial proportion of the town's 7,300 inhabitants and most of the resort accommodation, and the old town was becoming a business centre. The old town's compact, irregular and densely built-up area contrasted with the linear and more planned appearances of the new suburbs. A similar contrast between the old core and the new terraces on the outskirts is still discernible in many seaside resorts, for instance Scarborough in Yorkshire, Hastings in Sussex, and Weymouth in Dorset.(11) Building on the farmland was the only way in which the town could expand from the early 1780s because almost all of the land which was suitable for development in the old town had been built on. The continuing popularity of the town resulted in sustained building on the farmland from 1782, in order to provide all types of facilities, including workshops and private housing. At that time virtually all of the land within the parish, but outside the town, was farmland. Five open fields called Laines surrounded the town on its landward sides, four of which, Little, Hilly, North and West had boundaries impinging on the Steine or the old town. Only in West Laine did some enclosure precede building (Fig. 1). In the other laines all of the land was still owned as strips when it was built on and they left their imprint on the process of development and on the street pattern (Fig. 7).

Only a few other English towns, such as Portsmouth in Hampshire and Stamford in Lincolnshire had a similar extent of fossilised open fields surrounding them when they expanded.(12) Brighton's growth is of particular interest because of the way in which the demand for resort housing beside the sea or the resort facilities on the Steine influenced the growth of the suburbs. Land with the advantages of both attractions on the eastern side of the town was built on first and attracted the more expensive housing.

The system of landholding dictated the actual layout of the streets. The five laines were sub-divided into furlongs separated from one another by access paths called leakways, which usually became important east-west roads such as St. James's Street or Western Road (Fig. 7). Each furlong was divided into strips locally called paulpieces, which were owned in units called yardlands, most of which in 1780 comprised some seven acres held as about 20 specific paulpieces, with a stint for livestock on the pasture. The 84 yardlands were held by only eleven people, as a result of a process of consolidation extending over at least a century. Although enclosures of all the laines was considered during the 1770s, it did not take place and land was sold or let for building on long lease in strips which were often long but too narrow to build on. For instance, an auction in 1798 included a plot in Little Laine, Upper Furlong, 25 feet wide and 600 feet long, and another in North Laine, Second Furlong, the same width and 459 feet long.(13)

Compared with the development in the old town, building on the fields demanded more resources and organisation. The use of the paulpieces as the

Fig 7 BRIGHTON 1822

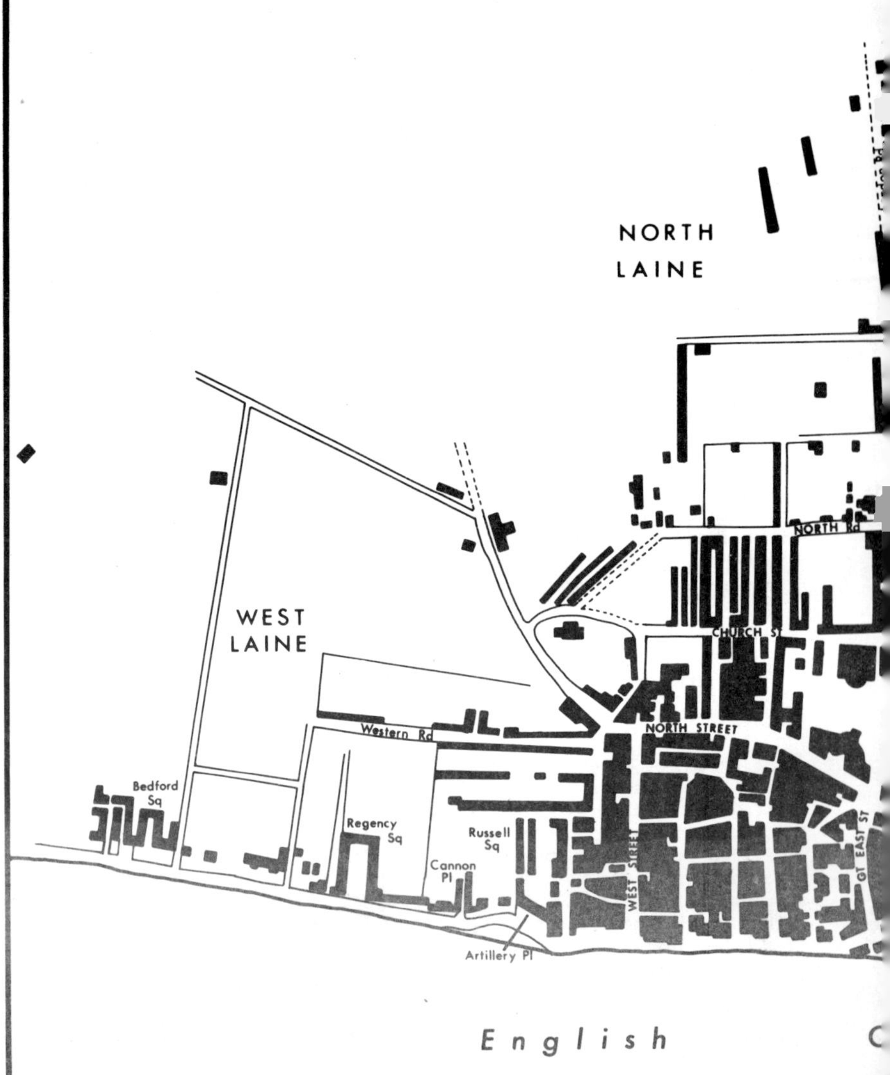

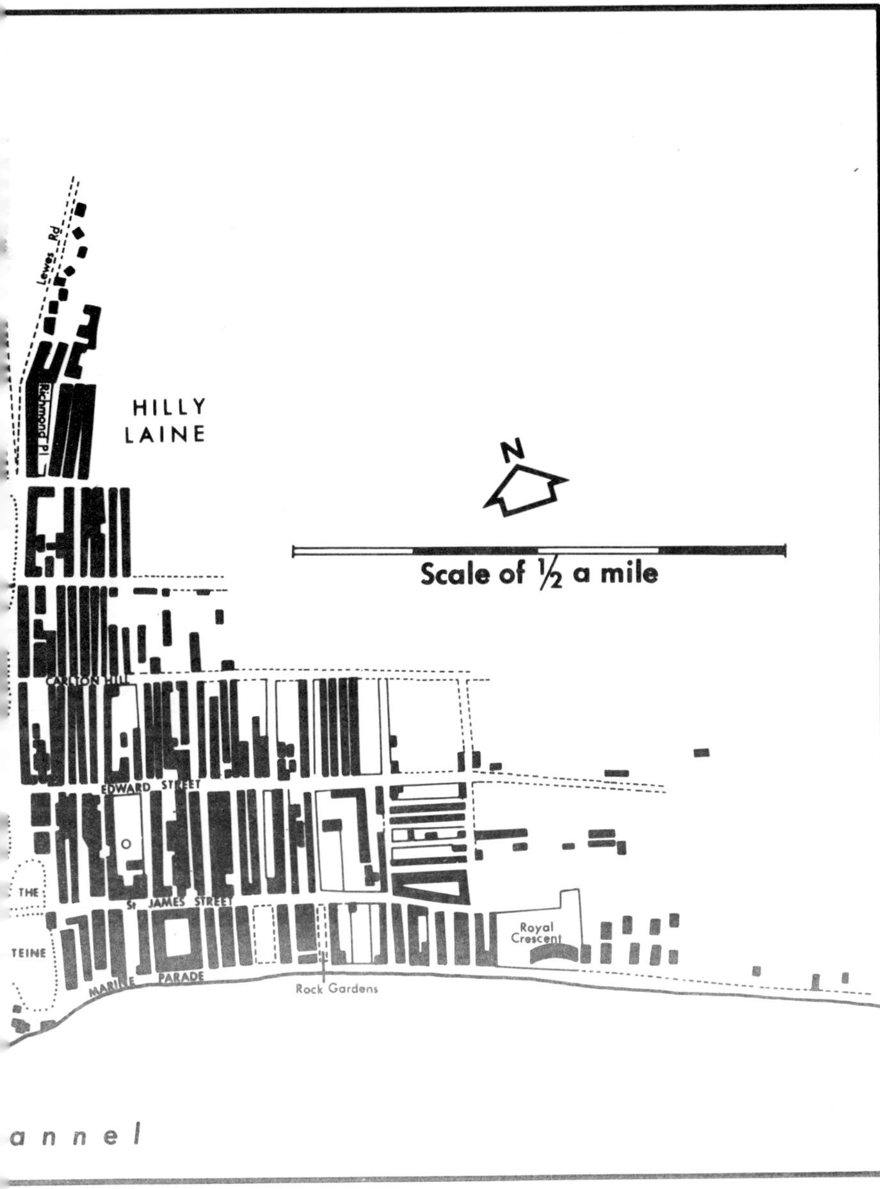
Lewes Rd
Richmond Pl
HILLY
LAINE
N
Scale of ½ a mile
CARLTON HILL
EDWARD STREET
St JAMES STREET
THE
TEINE
Royal
Crescent
MARINE PARADE
Rock Gardens
annel

basis for sales of land for development was the most effective way of converting the unenclosed agricultural land into building land, because attempting to build across the field system would have prolonged negotiations by involving more landowners and pieces of land. This practice did impose constraints upon development because the developer might have to buy several adjacent long narrow paulpieces in order to have a piece of land which was wide enough to build on. In order to use his land most effectively the developer would lay a road straight down its entire length, either down the middle, if there was sufficient land to allow for houses on both sides, or along one side with one row of houses. The next building project would then face the new road and its developer would be expected to widen it by dedicating part of his land as road. Roads were normally fifteen feet wide and this standard helped to make development easier and also more homogeneous. The need to lay roads down the length of the paulpieces in order that land in the middle had a right of way had an important effect on Brighton's street plan. Most of the developers assembled long but rectangular blocks of land which stretched the entire width of a furlong (Fig. 1), therefore the streets were laid straight and from one side of the furlong to the other. This practice ensured that the developer and his purchasers could use the leakways between the furlongs as rights of way, in order to reach their land and then proceed down the new street to their own plot and avoided disputes which could have arisen over access across other people's land. The leakways consequently became the main thoroughfares in the new suburbs.

Having assembled enough land for building and ensured adequate access to all of it the developer prepared to start his project. His decisions about the type and quality of buildings which he wished to build or wished others to build were influenced by how much money he had spent on purchasing the land, its location, the level of demand, how quickly he wished to dispose of it and whether he was intending to build and sell property or only to sell off building plots on which the purchasers would build. Land in favoured locations, such as near the Steine and the sea in Cliff Furlong in Little Laine, was the most expensive to buy and the developers expected to sell most of it to people who would then build houses to a minimum value and style specified in restrictive covenances contained in the deeds of conveyance or the lease. In these areas developers, such as Stephen Wood in Charles Street, sometimes built a few houses themselves in order to start off the project, but local people, particularly builders, then completed the project. Elsewhere developers were less concerned about setting the tone of the project and frequently sold all the land as building plots and without restrictive covenants and rapidly ceased to be involved.

Most of the streets of suburban Brighton were built as terraces which suited the layout of the blocks of paulpieces, saved building materials in a town where much had to be imported, including wood, stone and slates (although bricks were made at Wick) and made building easier and faster than the construction of detached or semi-detached houses, for the range of styles that were practical on the narrow plots was very restricted. The quality of buildings varied depending upon the location of the land and its cost, as well as the rigour with which the developer enforced the building covenants. The most expensive land which lay in a narrow band along the front of the Steine and on the cliff tops, had the most costly housing, for these areas were in demand for resort accommodation and the visitors' expectations of adequate space had to be fulfilled. Small plots with properties of only two storeys were typical of the areas of artisan housing and workshops on the north side of St. James's Street, where land was cheap because it was not wanted for resort housing. Thus a successful developer had to ensure that he had correctly assessed the potential of the area in which he was buying land for the type of development which he wished to undertake. If he paid too much for his land, then he would not find buyers at the price he wanted because they would purchase from his competitors either nearby or in another part of the town. In the early stages when the overall pattern of landuse which was to emerge was not yet discernible, development was particularly speculative because the developers could not look at what had already been built as a guideline for the potential of farmland close to it.(14)

The first laine to be developed was Little Laine, which was the nearest laine to East Street and had the Steine as its western boundary (Fig. 1). Little Laine was divided into two furlongs, Cliff and Upper which stretched along the cliff top as far east as Bedford Street. Terraces of houses were being built on western fringes of both furlongs where they looked on to the Steine when the Prince of Wales made his first visit to Brighton in 1783. In the mid-1780s German House and Place (now Madeira Place), Steine Street, Charles and Broad Streets were being built on Cliff Furlong along the cliff top between the Old Steine and what became Rock Gardens (on the south side of St. James's Street, which was previously the leakway separating Cliff from Upper Furlong). By 1792 almost all of Cliff Furlong was being developed. All of the streets were built at right angles to the cliff top, following the orientation of the paulpieces and extended the full width of the furlong (Fig. 5). The interest of fashionable visitors in sea air and in the social activities in the Steine area was reflected in the value of property which was on the cliff top but near to the Steine. The influence of these expectations is clear for Cliff Furlong, where the most expensive properties to buy or to rent were in Marine Parade along the cliff top and along the eastern side of the Old Steine (Fig. 5). The second most expensive lodging houses were in the most spacious streets in Cliff Furlong; New Steine, German Place and Broad Street. So important was a location by the sea of the Steine that most of the streets in Upper Furlong which lacked these advantages failed as resort development. (See below)

The development of Cliff Furlong in Little Laine illustrates how many Brighton people became involved in the building process and the speed with which paulpieces (strips) could be prepared for building on. Although eleven yardlanders held land in Little Laine in 1780 only one, John Hicks (of the old Ship Inn), attempted to be a developer. The rest of the yardlanders either sold their paulpieces or granted building leases which were normally of 99 years duration. Developers were so interested in land in this furlong that by 1792 at least 70 per cent was laid out ready for building on. A terrier of the open fields which was made in 1792 only notes that South Parade and the Royal Mews were build and lists the rest as though it was still farmland and belonged to the yardlanders. By 1792 several streets had begun and at least 17 people were involved as developers on this furlong, of whom 12 were gentlemen, in the professions or shopkeepers and five were builders. Of the 17, twelve lived in Brighton and five were described as Londoners, but one or two of these were probably resident in Brighton. Though some of them borrowed money in order to buy land, all of the Brightonians within this group were amongst the town's most prosperous citizens. The developers who were not builders, such as John Hall, a local doctor, normally had only one or two houses built for themselves by builders to set the tone of their project and sold the rest of the plots. The developers who were also builders, such as Stephen Wood and Thomas Howell, built more houses on their own land to sell or rent and sometimes built houses for clients who had already bought plots from them.(15)

The development of Charles and Broad Streets and German Place in Cliff

Furlong shows how strongly the layout and ownership of farmland influenced urban development. Charles Street was built across four paulpieces (strips), which gave Stephen Wood (a builder) a plot about 108 feet wide from east to west and 200 feet long from the cliff top leakway to the furlong's northern boundary, a leakway that became St. James's Street (Figs. 1,4,5). Wood purchased the freehold of two paulpieces but the rest was copyhold land let to him as leasehold by the yardlanders until after he had started to develop the street in the mid 1780s. Wood then managed to get the two copyhold paulpieces enfranchised. Broad Street was started by Thomas Howell on several paulpieces which were assembled in the same way as Charles Street's. Both developers were anxious to sell plots of land for building as freehold rather than leasehold because the price was higher, and this explains why they were willing to pay for enfranchisement if necessary. Both streets became rows of lodging and private houses. The covenants for Charles and Broad Streets probably specified the number of storeys and the minimum amount which purchasers of plots should spend on having a house built. The constraints of cost, plot size, the active interest of the developer and the style of housing which the developers had already built in order to set an example resulted in most houses having three storeys, a basement and garret and a small yard with a privy at the rear. Most of the houses had bow windows which gave more light and a greater feeling of spaciousness inside these narrow houses than inset ones would have. The facades were built of mathematical tiles or brick, or brick and flint. Stucco was sometimes used. Cobblestone fronts were not built in either of these streets but were in other streets in Little Laine. No sewers or properly made up roads were provided in the early streets and they were only paved by the Town Commissioners after all the houses were built. In streets built after circa 1800 some builders provided proper road surfaces with sewers for rain water run-off but the use of sewers for effluent was opposed by the Commissioners. Even in these upper class streets the contents of emptied cess pits and other waste was left in the street for the scavengers to collect.

The people who purchased houses or plots on which to build houses in Charles and Broad Streets were mostly local shopkeepers and craftsmen. Purchasers of plots normally paid cash and then some raised a mortgage on the value of the land in order to build a house, while others waited until they had sufficient capital themselves. These practices meant that streets were unfinished for long periods and even in 1792, when both Charles and Broad Streets had been under development for nearly 10 years and Wood and Howell had sold most of the land, only about six houses stood in each. In 1800 Charles Street had 13 houses and Broad Street 15 and several years elapsed before they were finally completed.(16)

German Place House (Fig. 4) was probably built as early as 1781-2, facing the sea and surrounded by its own grounds. John Daniel Richards, the owner, bought or leased nine paulpieces (strips) of land for his detached villa before rapid suburban development had started. In the late 1780s he began German Place, a terrace of lodging houses near to his own residence but following the typical north-south street pattern which was developing on the furlong. On Richard's death in 1791 his wife advertised the estate as a block of land suitable for house building. By then streets were being built on both its western and eastern sides. No-one was willing to purchase this prime site as a single block of land, it was too large for the typical Brighton developer who rarely speculated in anything more than one street at a time. In 1793 Mrs. Richards divided the land into small lots based on the pattern of the original paulpieces and buyers were soon found. For example Thomas Howell was able to buy a strip of land on which to build the east side of Broad Street. German Place (now Madeira Place) and the east side of

Fig 4 BRIGHTON 1788
1 Brighton Square (Knab)
2 Brighton Place
3 Old Ship
4 Steine Street
1 The Hempshares
0
yards
220
NORTH LAINE
HILLY LAINE
LITTLE LAINE
WEST LAINE
THE STEINE
NORTH PARADE
SOUTH PARADE
CHARLES ST
GERMAN PL
Pavilion
Castle Inn
Crawfords Library
Dr Russells House
Baths
Pool Valley
BLACK LION ST
SHIP ST
WEST STREET
NORTH STREET
CHURCH STREET

Camelford Street called (York Street) was built on the rest of the land. This land was too valuable for building high density terraced housing on to survive as the garden for a villa. A few more attempts were made to build detached villas elsewhere on the fields, for example in Rock Gardens and Egremont Place in Little Laine and along the cliff top in West Laine (Fig. 6). Most of them survived for only a few years before being demolished or submerged in a tide of terraced housing (Figs. 5,6).(17)

During the 1790s land at the western end of Cliff Furlong in East Laine (adjacent to Cliff Furlong in Little Laine) was bought by developers but most of it was not built on until the following decade. In 1799 a block of land which awaited houses stretched from Rock Gardens in Little Laine as far east as Royal Crescent in East Laine (Fig. 5). This area was not built on because the momentum of eastwards development slowed down during the late 1790s as the developers left their land on the town's eastern fringes dormant and concentrated upon existing building projects. The town's eastwards expansion apparently halted in the late 1790s because of the overprovision of land within existing streets on Cliff Furlong and competition from new projects which were started in the mid to later 1790s on land which was closer to the town in the Upper Furlong in Little Laine, and in Hilly and West Laines.

The apparent cessation in new projects on the eastern cliff top explains why Royal Crescent, the first project to be built in East Laine, appears to be so isolated as drawn on Cobby's map of the town in 1800 (Fig. 5). Royal Crescent was built on East Laine's Cliff Furlong where the paulpiece were orientated north to south. The Crescent is uncharacteristic of the eastern suburbs because it is built across the paulpieces in order to face the sea. The Crescent's generous layout can be partly explained by an accident of landownership as, unusually, the freehold of most of the land on which it was built was owned by one person, in order for a developer to own the entire block of land only one small but central paulpiece had to be purchased from another owner. Two other factors are also important. The first was that the project was started at a time when the town had temporarily reached its eastwards limits and land prices in this area may well have fallen, thus a crescent facing the sea was being built because the land was cheap in order to attract a clientele to this peripheral location. The second was that the developer, J.B. Otto, a West Indian plantation owner, did not have most of his money tied up in the Crescent and so could afford to take time developing it. Although the project was underway in 1799 and it is depicted on Cobby's map in 1800 none of the houses are listed in the Directory of 1800 and the first were probably completed circa 1800 to 1801. All of the houses were standing in 1809 when they were described as elegant but marred by their bow windows because of the loss of privacy. Not until circa 1814 when the houses were amongst the most highly valued in Brighton was the space between Rock Gardens and Royal Crescent infilled (as described below) and even as late as 1820 the Crescent marked the eastwards extent of continuous building along the East Cliff. Royal Crescent was one of the largest projects to be built on the fields before 1820 which was entirely financed by one person. It is also notable for the similarity of the houses (which have fronts made of mathematical tiles) and for having its own mews at the rear. There the land was only suitable for building services or low value housing because the sea view and air was blocked off by the Crescent.(18)

Competition from development in Brighton's other suburbs affected both the speed and the quality of the building between Rock Gardens and Royal Crescent. Although the development of the streets which infilled this area began between 1800 and 1809 (Fig. 6) and by 1814 only Grafton Street had not been named, the projects were more varied in quality than the rest of the streets on Little

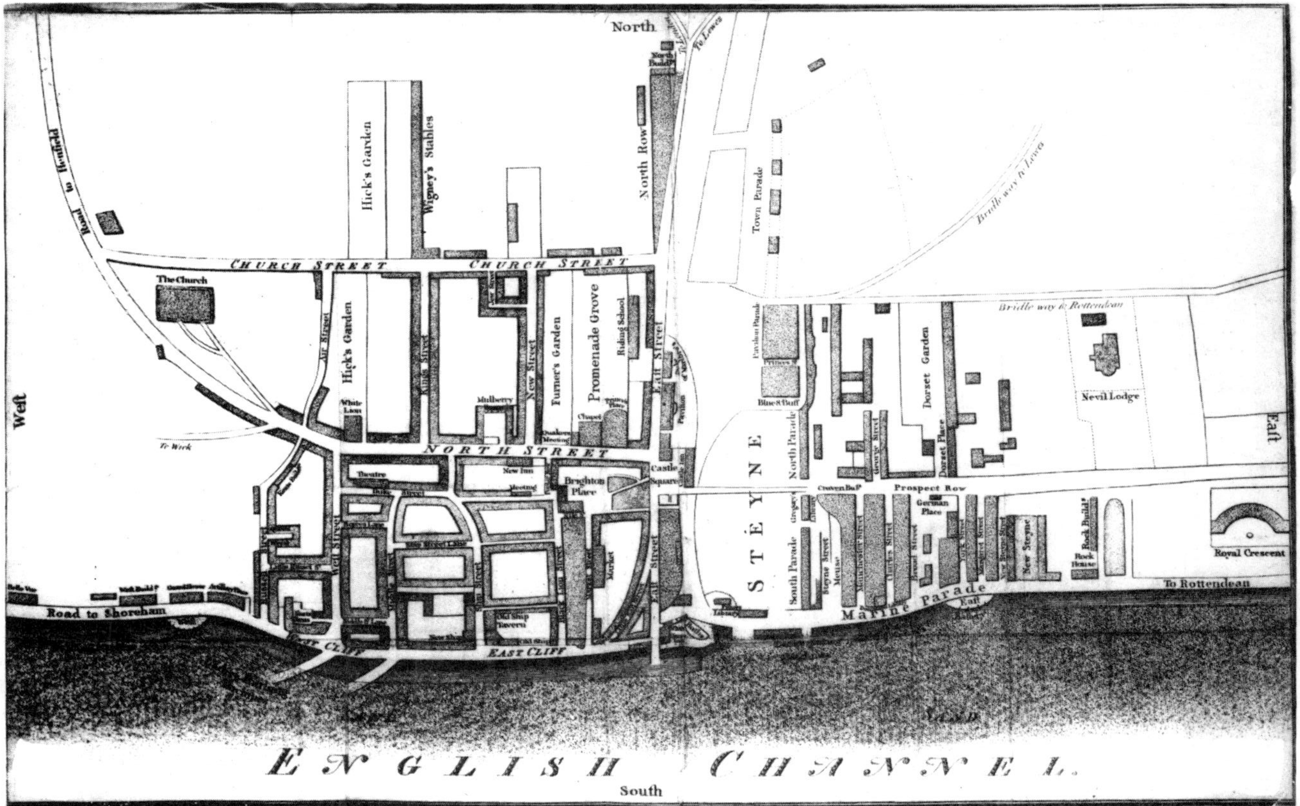

BRIGHTHELMSTON.

Laine. Indeed, the low valuations of many properties in this area in 1814 suggests that the developers relaxed their control on the land in order to dispose of the plots. (19)

Upper Furlong, Little Laine: the first suburban service area

By contrast with the rapid development of upper class lodging houses on Cliff Furlong in Little Laine, Upper Furlong in the same laine, but between St. James's Street and Edward Street developed more slowly (Figs. 1,5). Most of the streets in Upper Furlong which lacked the advantages of a location by the sea or the Steine failed as resort development and were being developed as artisan housing and workshops by 1800. The only successful upper class housing on Upper Furlong, North and Pavilion Parades, was built in the early 1780s along its short western fringe and facing the Steine. Developers displayed little interest in the rest of Upper Furlong until after 1792 because projects on Cliff Furlong were still being laid out. From 1792 there was increasing interest in Upper Furlong because most of the land in Cliff Furlong had been sold for development and developers hoped to build the same type of property. By 1792 land in Upper Furlong was being laid out as upper class streets in imitation of Cliff Furlong. Only Craven Buildings, Prospect Row and Dorset Gardens were built to the quality the developers originally intended. By 1798 they had turned from the failure to establish high quality projects to meeting the rapidly growing demand for housing and workplaces for shopkeepers, craftsmen and their employees. George Street, Cumberland and High Streets were all begun before 1800 by developers who had originally intended to build more superior projects. Lower quality projects were soon successful and George Street, for example, was built up in seven years, faster than many upper class streets. There was very little building control exerted over any of these streets and consequently landuse was very mixed; the 1814 rate book lists in George Street: mews, a pub with its own brewhouse and workshops, and these were intermixed with housing that had a greater range of valuations than was normal in better quality streets on the seafront. Infilling behind the street fronts was common on Upper Furlong because the plots along the street were small in order to encourage high density development because this method of development made low quality buildings profitable. By 1807 the land to the west of George Street was occupied by St. James's Court and Row, Little George Street and Howell's almshouse. The development of St. James's Street from about 1804 as the shopping centre for the fashionable houses on Cliff Furlong (on its southern side) stimulated building on Upper Furlong where many craftsmen and retailers had their workshops and warehouses. (20)

As early as 1822 some streets on Upper Furlong were becoming notorious for prostitutes and disturbances and frequently reported by the nightwatch. By 1822 development on Hilly Laine to the north and on East Laine to the east had hemmed in the Upper Furlong and this contributed towards the deterioration of most of the development upon it although St. James's Street continued to be an important shopping centre. From 1840 most of the streets on the Upper Furlong were identified in Health Reports as being serious threats to public health. Thus the initial role of the area as a 'service' zone combined with the low quality of the development over most of it, contributed to its environmental decline. (21)

Suburban development inland, on Hilly and North Laines

The importance of a location beside the sea or the Steine and the orientation of the paulpieces influenced the development of Hilly and North Laines. Both had the Steine as a boundary, but neither were by the sea (Fig. 1). Their paulpieces were orientated north-south and consequently building houses which faced the sea was not easily achieved. The location of development on both laines was also influenced by their topography, for their flattest and most sheltered land was nearest to the Steine, in the valley bottom between the two laines (both of which lay principally upon the valley's side, see Fig. 1). The importance of proximity to the old town or the Steine was also an incentive to building on the south-eastern corner of North Laine and the south-western corner of Hilly Laine, where the flattest land lay and this explains the triangular pattern of development on both laines which is discernible on Figs. 1, 4 and 5.

Development on Hilly Laine began when the western side of Little Laine was built up. By 1799 Town Parade was being built on the south-western corner of Hilly Laine, looking across the Steine towards the Pavilion, but building progressed slowly (Fig. 5). Due to the continued availability of land elsewhere for town housing, particularly in Little Laine and West Laine on the sea front, the pace of development of similar housing along the fringe of Hilly Laine was slow. Not until most of the streets on Little Laine were partially built up by about 1804-5, did progress on Hilly Laine speed up, yet Town Parade was still incomplete in 1804 when the first houses in Carlton Place to the north (which was started in 1804) were ready to sell. Both terraces were almost complete when Richmond Terrace and Albion Place were being built father north in 1807. Building up the rest of the fringe of Hilly Laine took longer, the development of the land which separated Carlton Place from Richmond Terrace was started by 1808 but few houses were built until after 1815. North of Richmond Terrace, Waterloo Place was not started until 1819, nor Hanover Terrace until after 1820. The slow rate of development (compared with Little Laine or the cliff frontage of West Laine)reflected the disadvantage of distance from the sea and the town itself and being in a valley which was becoming a busy thoroughfare.(22)

On the main part of Hilly Laine the distinctive triangular pattern of development noted earlier began to emerge from 1804. The first developers had already been responsible for the development of the service area in Upper Furlong in Little Laine, which was just on the south side of Edward Street (the leakway that separated the two laines). At first developers attempted to build resort housing and some even bought large numbers of paulpieces so that they could build terraces across the ends of the strips to face the sea, but the quality of development quickly became the same as on Upper Furlong in Little Laine: artisan streets. Between 1804 and 1808 there was a minor building boom on Hilly Laine during which a cluster of streets which were slums by 1840 were partially built, including Carlton, Nelson, John and Thomas Streets. From 1808 building continued more sedately and few new streets were started. In 1814 half-finished streets of artisan housing and workshops were scattered all along the lower slopes of the laine behind the upper class terraces. Most of the developers found that land took a long time to sell, sometimes several years, and were anxious to let it meanwhile. Although local farmers were uninterested in renting small areas that were intermixed with housing, the plots were suitable for other landuses which were always found on the fringes of Georgian towns such as limekilns, stables and paddocks, cowhouses and market gardening. Well into the 1820s the pattern of 'town fringe' landuses and partly finished streets was characteristic of the outer parts of this laine. Although the pace of development on Little Laine had been too rapid for a fringe of temporary landuses as described on Hilly Laine to become established the same phenomena did occur on North Laine where the rate and pattern of urban development was comparable to Hilly Laine's.

The pattern and sequence of development on North Laine (Fig. 1) was influenced not only by the negative aspects of its location for resort development (which were the same as for Hilly Laine), but also by a positive aspect, proximity to the old town and particularly closeness to North Street and Castle Square which was a busy and prosperous shopping centre and thoroughfare from the 1780s.(23)

The earliest building development on North Laine was North Row which was started in 1772 on the laine's south-eastern corner, facing the Steine. The rate of building was very slow and North Row consisted largely of service buildings as well as the King and Queen Inn. Progress on North Row was hindered by the development of the very substantial crofts on the north side of North Street, which were built on from the early 1770s. By 1780 roads which had been laid through the crofts to link North Street and Church Street made access from the old town to North Laine easy. The crofts between North and Church Streets provided workshops and cheaper housing for the businesses in North Street but from the 1770s these buildings displaced stabling, paddocks and large gardens northwards onto the first furlong of North Laine. In the late 1790s when the crofts were built over, urban development really started on North Laine with upper class housing along its eastern fringe and accommodation for services such as workshops and cheaper housing over the rest of the land. This pattern was similar to the development of Hilly Laine and continued until the 1830s.

However, in 1800 only a few buildings had been completed on North Laine and the pace of development lagged behind the other laines. In 1800 along the Steine's fringe the northern end of North Row, consisted of lodging houses and extended as far north as Gloucester Place. Only a few buildings stood on the first furlong and they consisted of a few small rows of cottages along Church Street, Wigneys Stables and Hick's Gardens (later Spring Gardens) and a row of buildings along what eventually became the east side of Tichbourne Street. By 1808 a street pattern had emerged on the first furlong between the two leakways (fieldpaths) on its southern and northern boundaries which became Church Street and North Road. Building had also begun on the eastern end of second furlong where St. George's Place, Cheltenham Place and Kensington Gardens were under way. Building along the Steine fringe was progressing northwards faster than development on the Laine as whole, for Gloucester Place and Trafalgar Place were already being built by 1808 (Fig. 6) and building had also started on North Butts on the eastern side of London Road where houses in Oxford Place were for sale. Between 1808 and 1820 ribbon development up the London Road continued while earlier developments were infilled.

From the 1790s the increasing pressure on space in the old town and the rising demand for goods resulted in the displacement of old established crafts, such as blacksmithing northwards into North Laine and the development of specialist crafts that were new to this town, such as iron-founding on the laine rather than in the old town. The large number of stables and paddocks for horses in North Laine probably helped to provide a basis for the metal trades because making horseshoes, harnessing and repair work to waggons and stage coaches provided business.

The clustering of workshops on North Laine which had developed by 1820 is characteristic of early nineteenth century towns, and was convenient for specialisation in different stages of manufacture such as in furniture making or coach building. Most of the workshops and Brighton's largest manufacturing concern, the Regent Foundry were also developed on North Laine

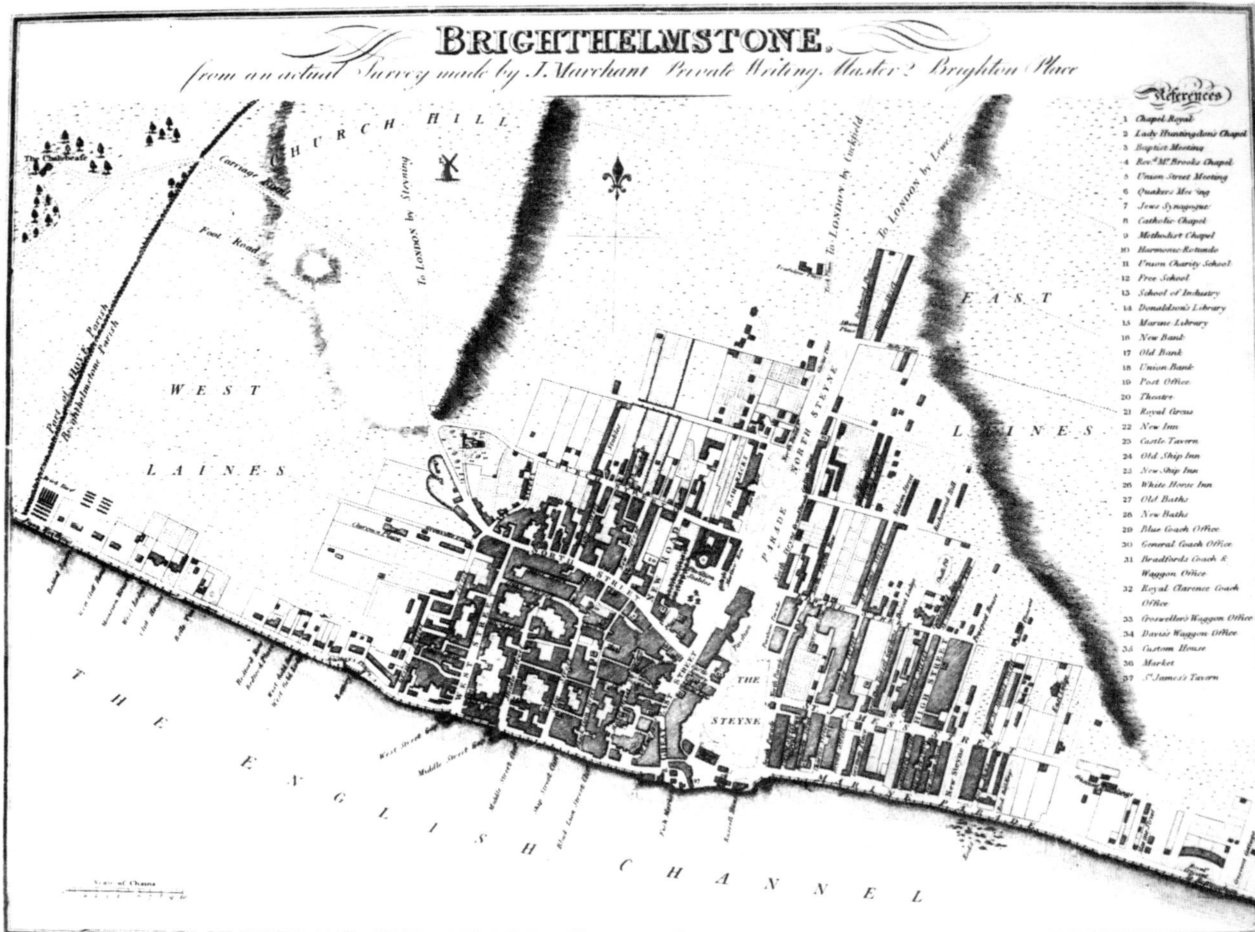
BRIGHTHELMSTONE,
from an actual Survey made by J. Marchant Private Writing Master, Brighton Place
References
1 Chapel Royal
2 Lady Huntingdon's Chapel
3 Baptist Meeting
4 Revd. Mr. Brooks Chapel
5 Union Street Meeting
6 Quakers Meeting
7 Jews Synagogue
8 Catholic Chapel
9 Methodist Chapel
10 Harmonic Rotundo
11 Union Charity School
12 Free School
13 School of Industry
14 Donaldson's Library
15 Marine Library
16 New Bank
17 Old Bank
18 Union Bank
19 Post Office
20 Theatre
21 Royal Circus
22 New Inn
23 Castle Tavern
24 Old Ship Inn
25 New Ship Inn
26 White Horse Inn
27 Old Baths
28 New Baths
29 Blue Coach Office
30 General Coach Office
31 Bradfords Coach & Waggon Office
32 Royal Clarence Coach Office
33 Croswellers Waggon Office
34 Davis's Waggon Office
35 Custom House
36 Market
37 St. James's Tavern
CHURCH HILL
Carriage Road
Foot Road
To LONDON by Steyning
To LONDON by Cuckfield
To LONDON by Lewes
EAST LAINES
WEST LAINES
Part of Hove Parish
Brighthelmstone Parish
NORTH STEYNE
PARADE
THE STEYNE
NORTH STREET
WEST STREET
EAST STREET
NEW ROAD
HIGH STREET
ST. JAMES'S STREET
MARINE PARADE
West Street Gap
Middle Street Gap
Ship Street Gap
Black Lion Street Gap
THE ENGLISH CHANNEL
Scale of Chains

because of cheap land and access to shops and other services in North Street which gave them their business. As on Hilly Laine purchasers of land for development in North Laine were often over-optimistic. By 1814 land by the parish boundary at the north end of North Laine was used for market gardening, which suggests that it was awaiting buyers for building but that there was a long time lag before buyers were found. The other landuses noted on Hilly Laine were also found on North Laine and for the same reasons.

The development of West Laine

The pattern of development in most of West Laine was different from the other laines because ownership was much less fragmented.(24) The rate of development was slow compared with Little Laine, for despite its coastal location, West Laine was distant from the resort facilities. In the 1780s and 90s, only the three furlongs which were close to the town and which were held as paulpieces (as in the other laines), were built on. Of these, most of the two furlongs adjacent to West Street were developed as Russell Street and as housing for people employed in the town. Because of its prime site on the cliff top and shallow depth back from the cliff, Cliff Butts was used for short terraces such as Artillery Place (1793), and detached villas facing the sea (Belle Vue, 1794). This development produced a layout which contrasted with the development on the cliff east of the town in Little Laine. In the early 1790s, Thomas Kemp, one of the three owners of the remaining furlongs in West Laine made purchases from, or exchanges with, the other two owners (the Western family and the Duke of Dorset) which gave Kemp the sole ownership of most of West Laine. Kemp was then able to lease or sell blocks of land which offered greater flexibility of layout for development than did strips.

Large scale building on West Laine began after 1800 when most of Cliff Furlong in Little Laine had been developed and the accelerating growth of the town stimulated interest in using land on the town's western side for resort accommodation as an alternative to extending the town farther east into East Laine. Between 1801 and 1808 Kemp released all of the land west of Cliff Butts as far as the parish boundary with Hove for development. At first more houses facing the sea were built, including West Cliff Lodge which was described in 1802 as built of brick and stone with wings and gothic and sash windows. But, almost at the western end of the parish Bedford Square was started in circa 1801. This was Brighton's first Georgian square and the first major project in the suburbs which did not involve purchasing land from more than one owner. Its very peripheral location may explain why only 12 of the 36 houses planned had been built by 1814 although the surge in building development on West Laine before 1820 resulted in its completion by 1818 (Fig. 6).

As building on Little Laine (to the east of the old town) neared completion in about 1810 so interest in lodging house development in West Laine increased further, and this resulted in a greater demand for land for the development of terraced housing. The development along the length of Cliff Butts was an impediment to building fashionable terraced housing on the land behind because access to the seafront was blocked. Hence most of the rows of villas and terraces along the cliff top depicted in the maps of 1800 and 1808 (Figs. 5 and 6) were soon demolished in order to provide roads to the land north of Cliff Butts. From 1810 squares and streets of lodging houses were developed on West Laine, including Cannon Place (1813) and Regency Square (1817). Most of them had the benefit of more gardens and greater floor areas than the streets on Little Laine because of the freedom from the constraints that were imposed by building over the paulpieces in Little Laine. Inland on

West Laine even the more modest housing such as Blucher (1806), Clarence (1807) and Grenville (1809?) Places which were occupied by less affluent visitors and by prosperous local tradesmen were more spacious than housing of comparable status on the town's eastern side.

Even by 1820 only a small part of West Laine had been built on, and the majority of the buildings in West Laine post date 1820 from when Kemp deliberately sold large amounts of land for upper class housing development. The development on much of Kemp's land in West Laine was contemporary to Kemp and Brunswick Towns and larger in scale and more classical in design than the developments which were begun before 1820. The only artisan area in West Laine was built by 1810 between Russell and West Streets. Although the development of the three tenantry furlongs was influenced by the orientation of paulpieces and their ownership, the extent of the influence was significantly less than in Little Laine. This was partly because most of the individual's holdings in West Laine were larger than in Little Laine but it was also because of the slow rate of development which allowed developers to accrue bigger portions of the furlongs. This also permitted some flexibility in layout in West Laine which the pressure and rate of development on Little Laine did not allow.

By 1800 at least a third of Brighton's houses stood in the suburbs on the open fields and perhaps two thirds of them were either let as lodging houses or used as lodgings. The majority of the town's 7,339 inhabitants still lived within the old town. Between 1801 and 1811 the number of houses rose from 1,420 to 2,380, or by 61 per cent, and as 80 houses were also being built in 1811, the rate of building was about commensurate with the increase in population. By 1811 the suburbs contained over half the town's housing and a large proportion of its population. Between 1811 and 1821 the rate of building dramatically accelerated and many streets which had been started before 1800 were completed.(25) By 1821 the suburbs probably housed two thirds of the town's population, a remarkable alteration in the balance between the old and new areas.

By 1808 the town was roughly triangular in outline with its base along the coast and its apex at North Steine, and by 1820 building on West Laine had accentuated the shape (Figs. 6 and 7). In 1820 most of Brighton's buildings were under 30 years old. East Street and the south-western side of the Old Steine soon began to lose their importance in the 1820s when resort facilities such as baths and libraries were built within the suburbs.(26) From about 1820 the development of estates of villas and large terraced houses, such as Kemp Town to the east of Brighton, Brunswick Town (Hove), and the Montpellier area of Brighton which were intended to provide space for entertaining in the home, signalled the changed attitude of the wealthy towards seaside resorts and a new stage of Brighton's development.(27)

5. POPULATION AND EMPLOYMENT 1750 TO 1825

Between 1750 and 1821 Brighton's population increased from about 2,000 to just over 24,400. Of the resorts, only Bath's population grew faster. Brighton's population increased faster than those of northern industrial towns whose populations were twice as big (about 4,000) in 1750, such as Blackburn, Bolton and Oldham. Many county towns whose populations were two or three times as big as Brighton's was in 1750, such as Canterbury, Salisbury, Warwick and Worcester, were considerably smaller than Brighton in

1821. The population of Lewes and Chichester, the county towns of East and West Sussex, had been larger than Brighton's in 1750 but in 1821 both towns had only about 7,000 inhabitants.(1)

Why did Brighton's development as a resort result in a population growth rate which was faster than many British towns? The answer seems to be that this town's exceptional success as a fashionable resort resulted in a level of expenditure by visitors which provided outstanding opportunities for employment. The resort facilities and activities described in Chapter 3 did not employ many people and so by themselves would not have resulted in population increase, but they attracted the visitors and encouraged them to stay in the town and to spend money while here on other things such as food, accommodation, clothes, luxury goods and travel, all of which generated employment. As the number of visitors rose, the average length of stay increased and the season extended so, as in a modern resort, the size of the population which could depend upon the visitors for their livelihood increased. Conversely, the speed at which the town became a successful resort and its continued growth, was partially dependant upon the successful provision of the facilities which visitors expected, including not only resort facilities and luxury shops, but also basic necessities and suitable accommodation.

Between 1750 and 1780 the town's employment structure was profoundly altered by the transition from seafaring town to seaside resort. In 1750 there was only a limited range of occupations because of the town's poverty and the lack of a regional clientele due to the nearness of Lewes, the county town. (2) The crafts represented in Brighton included ropemakers and ship-wrights, who supplied the town's maritime needs, and blacksmiths, cordwainers, joiners and tailors for domestic requirements. The limited number of retailers reflected the low level of expenditure within the town, for they provided only basic necessities: brewer, baker, innkeeper, haberdasher. The town's teacher represented the professions.

From 1750 the variety and number of occupations increased and reflects the rise in demand for trades and services which the change of function from maritime to watering place brought. It is possible to detect two stages in the development of employment which match those described in Chapter 3, the first from 1750 to 1780 and the second from 1781. The increase in employment and the growth of population in each phase were closely linked.

Between 1750 and 1780 trades and services which were common in most busy small towns of the time were attracted to Brighton; linendrapers, tanners, tallowchandlers, plumbers, cabinetmakers, grocers, drapers. There was also a rapid increase in the number of people who offered the basic services and trades that the town already had, such as innkeepers, malsters, bakers, carpenters. Most small towns had one or two of the more specialist employments, such as perukemakers, a hatter, a milliner and these soon arrived, so did some professions such as more schoolmasters, doctors, surgeons. By 1780 because of its resort function, the town supported a wider range of luxury trades and services and professions than would normally be expected in a town of this size, including a gold and silver smith, cutlers, librarians, portrait painters, jeweller, doctors, surgeons and apothecaries, boarding schools and teachers.(3)

Many of the new occupations which Brighton had by 1780 were established by people who came from the surrounding region, especially from Lewes. Because of years of poverty most of Brighton's inhabitants in the 1750s and 1760s lacked the expertise and the money to start new businesses. The town had so little skilled labour at first that most skilled people had to be recruited from elsewhere. Local people were employed in semiskilled or unskilled work, or tasks which required little training, such as working in an inn, or being a general domestic servant, and so initially the numbers of inhabitants who found new jobs were probably quite small. Although the town's population was rising even in 1750 the large number of people who received aid from the Overseers of the Poor until the late 1760s suggests that opportunities for semi and unskilled employment did not keep pace. By 1780 the town's continued success resulted in plenty of suitable jobs for the townsfolk and encouraged immigration by young people from the region. Immigration triggered off a further increase in the rate of population growth which became faster than the national average, even though the period from 1780 to 1821 was a period of outstanding increase nationally. From 1780 London tradesmen were attracted to the town, some opened branch shops for the season, others moved their entire businesses.

The major reason why Brighton's development as a resort resulted in such a population growth rate was that nearly all the goods and services which inhabitants wanted were made or provided within the town. Even in 1821 the increased volume and range of mass produced consumer goods made available by industrialisation in Britain had done little to reduce the importance of local production of many goods in most towns but especially in resorts, where wealthy people expected their individual needs to be catered for. Thus the visitors directly provided employment for dressmakers, shoemakers, milliners, jewellers. Their liking for the town provided employment in the building and furniture trades, especially because of the large number of houses which were built to be let as furnished lodging houses or used as lodgings which meant that furnished rooms were let to visitors. Catering for visitors provided employment for butchers, bakers and confectioners, also for wholesalers who supplied livestock, flour and other foodstuffs and for 'eating houses' (restaurants).(4) Domestic servants were employed by the visitors and by many townsfolk who did well from the town's prosperity. By 1780 the town's population was becoming very prosperous and this also stimulated population increase because residents spent more on goods and services within the town and so contributed to the demand for goods and labour.

From the 1780s trade directories help to show how the town's specialist function influenced its employment structure (Table 5.1) even though only one of them lists people who let accommodation. Amongst the shortcomings from which directories suffer as a source for studying occupational structure three have special significance in resort towns. First, entries had to be paid for. Second, certain trades and services tend to be over-represented because they are more directly dependent upon the people who use directories. Third, the selectivity exercised by the compiler, unfortunately the exclusion of accommodation is a major limitation.(5) The importance of accommodation is indicated by Cobby's Directory of 1800. Nearly two-fifths of the people listed in entries in Cobby's Directory are there solely because they owned lodgings or lodging houses to let. In addition a significant group also had other occupations. This sector must have been a major source of employment for servants. It was very important to the building trades, for, like all expanding towns in this period, Brighton had a large number of people who were employed in supplying building materials and in the actual building industry such as bricklayers, plumbers, glaziers.(6)

Even though accommodation is excluded the service sector employed two fifths of the people listed in the directories. The town's major manufacturing employment was heavily dependent upon the visitors for it consisted mainly of making clothes, food processing, furniture and coaches and harness. The building sector was also quite large, reflecting the town's growth. Compared

Table 5.1 Brighton Employment by Occupational Sectors from Directories 1783-1824 (11)

SECTOR	YEAR AND PERCENTAGE EMPLOYED IN EACH SECTOR			
	1784 %	1793 %	1800 %	1824 %
Professions	29	16	14	12
Services excluding accommodation				
Distributive and Personal	29	24	31	35
Transport	2	8	3	3
Inns	8	10	10	4
All Services (excl. acc'n)	39	42	44	42
Manufacturing - Food	10	5	6	5
Clothing	2	13	12	15
Other	14	10	14	13
All Manufacturing	26	28	32	33
Building	6	13	8	11
Agriculture	-	1	2	2
TOTAL (100%)	51	340	474	2090
Total above as % of all entries in directory	-	84	61	81
Accommodation % all entries	-	3	37	2
Commercial % all entries			1	1
Private income % all entries	-	13	1	16
All entries (100%)	51	407	774	2560
Number families	690(est)	1230(est)	1390(1801)	5580(est)
Population (year)	3620(1784)	5669(1794)	7339(1801)	29300(est)
Possible number of families represented (%)		33%	50%	40%

est = estimate

with industrial towns Brighton's manufacturing sector was small and strikingly dependent upon local demand. Nothing was produced for sale on the national market or within the region. Most English county towns had a better developed industrial and commercial sector.

The selectivity of directories can be useful when seeking to identify where fashionable visitors shopped, for businesses in fashionable streets normally chose to be included in directories. As the town expanded so new shopping areas developed and the older ones changed in character. Although before 1821 only Cobby's Directory of 1800 gives addresses, Baxter's Directory of 1822 and his fuller 1824 edition help to show where new areas developed during the town's phase of resort development from 1780.(7) In the 1780s and 1790s Castle Square and the eastern end of North Street became the town's fashionable shopping centre and East Street specialised increasingly in high quality food shops. By the mid 1790s people who described themselves as high class drapers, such as George Elmore, were coming from London to establish businesses and settled in North Street and Castle Square. Dressmakers and other fashion traders came to Brighton for the season from prestigious London shopping streets, such as Bond Street. By 1793 Brighton had a wider range of services advertised in the Universal Directory of that year than Lewes and the county town's role as the developer of trades and services in Brighton had been supplanted by London.(8)

In 1800 Cobby's Directory confirms how important North Street and Castle Square had become, especially near the Steine where the road was filled by coaches going to the inns and passengers waiting at the coach offices, and the town's banks, branches of fire insurance offices, larger shops and town houses were intermixed. Although East Street had high class confectioners and bakers, as well as fashionable milliners, tailors and breeches-makers, Market Street was the main street for food shops particularly porkmen, poulterers, cowmen and butchers, because of the nearness to the market where meats and dairy products were also sold. Ship Street was already becoming a street of solicitors' offices. There were few services or trades in the suburbs. In the early 1800s employment in services and trades became more dispersed although the professions continued to remain clustered in the 'old town'. By 1810 St. James's Street had become the shopping centre for the new suburbs on the eastern side of the Steine and by 1822 (and in 1824) the range of shops at the western end of the street near the Steine were similar in status to those in North Street, although fewer in number.

The directories reveal a striking change in the locational pattern of basic services and trades between 1800 and 1822/24. By the latter dates although North Street was still the dominant shopping centre and the market area dominated the fresh food trades, other shops for the townsfolk had developed. Little shops opened in the streets to the north of North Street and St. James's Street (Fig. 7) where many people worked in the workshops which supplied the retailers on the main shopping streets. By 1820 retailing and workshops were being separated by their owners because of the high rents on main street frontages but the relationship between retailers and workshops was also changing as the retailers ceased to maintain their own workshops and sent their business to workshops owned by craftsmen who supplied more than one retailer.(9)

Georgian Brighton was a 'service town' where population was dependant upon the town's popularity as a resort and on seasonal expenditure by visitors for its employment. All sectors of the employed population were vulnerable to seasonal unemployment and reduced earnings when the number of visitors fell. That Brighton's population grew so quickly is a very eloquent testimonial to her success as a resort and the employment which this could generate. (10)

6. ADMINISTRATION c.1740 TO 1820

Until 1773 the vestry was the town's only administrative body but from 1773 the organization of the town's administration became increasingly complex because town commissioners were appointed. The major changes are shown in Tables 6.1A to 6.1C which show how the commissioners become responsible for the conduct of most of the town's affairs.

Between 1740 and 1820 the town remained within the bounds of the parish of Brighton which was the basis for both civil and ecclesiastical administration (Fig. 1). Until 1773 the vestry, which theoretically consisted of all of the householders who paid parish rates was responsible for the conduct of most parish affairs including: the annual appointment from amongst themselves of the churchwardens, the overseers of the poor and the surveyor of highways; levying parish rates and the supervision of the accounts of all parish officers including the constable's. The parish beadle (if there was one) and the master of the workhouse were both paid employees of the vestry. By the 1770s the increasingly influential post of clerk to the vestry was filled by a solicitor who probably charged a fee, and the status of the post had changed from being an annual obligation to a prestigeous position because of the increasing importance of the vestry's role in town affairs in this period as representatives of the rate payers. (1)

Although the constable and his assistants the headboroughs were nominated from amongst the ratepayers and the constable was an important member of the vestry these officials were appointed annually by a court leet. This was a meeting of local worthies from the parishes of Brighton, Patcham and East Blatchington all of which belonged to the Hundred of Whalesbone. The court leet of the hundred (the group of parishes) had once functioned as a court for petty offences and had appointed several officials but by 1750 the only offices which survived were constable and the headboroughs. By 1750 the constable was always a resident ratepayer in Brighton and his importance in the town increased as the town developed. The court leet was traditionally summoned by the Earl of Abergavenny's steward and should have met annually on Easter Monday to appoint the new officers. It was only infrequently convened and consequently, in some years the local Justices of the Peace to whom the constable was accountable confirmed the appointments of him and his helpers. Presumably a list of nominees was then presented by the vestry. (2)

The parish paid land and window taxes to the government but although residents in the town were normally appointed as tax assessors and collectors they were neither responsible to nor controlled by the parish. By 1770 there was an excise officer and riding officers who were appointed by the Board of Customs and were also employees of the government. (3)

Between 1750 and 1773 (during the first twenty years of the town's development as a resort), no one was responsible for the regulation of important aspects of town life such as street cleansing, lighting, paving, the prevention of nuisances and minimal controls over building construction such as the prohibition of combustible roof materials (e.g. thatch). Not until the late 1700s was there a resident justice of the peace. Because the town lacked a local court who could deal with petty offenders until Petty Sessions were started there in about 1812, offenders had to be taken to the Petty Sessions at Lewes, even though Brighton was the largest town in Sussex from about 1800. The court leet, had it remained active, could have made and enforced by-laws which would have regulated the streets and acted as a local court for petty offences. In some towns which developed rapidly from the mid-eighteenth century, for example Manchester, the court leet still operated.(4)

The vestry was not obliged to regulate the town and did not choose to do so and consequently the business which they conducted was the same as that in a rural parish, the care of the poor, some maintenance of highways and keeping the parish church in repair.

The membership of the vestry reflected the town's poverty. Between 1744 and 1761, 12 men were required annually to fulfill all the parochial offices and two more to act as the King's tax collectors. Although the population was about 2000 in the 1740s and increased thereon, between 1744 and 1761 there were only about 100 ratepayers. If women, minors, old men and absentee ratepayers are excluded, the total number of men who could serve was small. The annual lists of parish officers to 1761 suggests that only about 50 families provided the incumbents but a small number of men held posts frequently which provided both continuity and the opportunity to develop a tightly controlled select vestry.(5) By the late eighteenth century, vestry officials only consulted the remaining taxpayers by calling open meetings over which the constable presided.(6) The most frequent post holders in the 1750s were men who held a lot of property in the town and benefitted from the town's increasing prosperity from 1750.(7)

Until 1810 when the Directors and Guardians of the Poor took it over, the vestry's main responsibility was the care of the town's poor (Table 6). Between 1744 and 1761 the total sum collected from the poor rate was always between £200 and £300 but although more than 450 town properties were eligible for rating in 1744 only 115 were not exempt. The large number of unrated town properties (75%) is indicative of the low value of land in the town before resort development began.(8) Until 1810 the poor rate was collected and administered by the Overseers of the Poor but the expenditure was controlled by the vestry who were representatives of the town's ratepayers and took a keen interest in this major expense. By 1750 the poor rate had been augmented on several occasions by the justices of the peace for the county who first levied a rate on parishes surrounding Brighton and when this imposition was opposed, levied a rate on the county.(9) The overseers provided help for the poor in several ways. Weekly allowances were paid to applicants who remained in their own homes. Though in most places this practice was only intended to relieve seasonal unemployment, in Brighton payments were probably made for long periods until resort development began to provide employment. Help in kind was given to families and to individuals who did not qualify for regular payments but who needed periodic help with clothing, coal, food or medical care or a contribution towards the cost of burying a relative. The parish's workhouse and town hall on Bartholomews took the sick, aged and young, and the inmates were expected to work if they were fit enough to, and make their own clothes and prepare the food. In the 1740s the workhouse inmates picked oakum but by the 1780s mackerel nets were made for sale. The overseers appointed a workhouse master or mistress and put out to contract the supply of food and medical care. The number of inmates probably fluctuated depending on the time of year and the amount of employment but in 1761 there were about 35 people. As the town grew so the numbers who needed help increased although they were probably a much smaller proportion of the total population and consisted mainly of people who, due to

Table 6.1 The Development of Brighton's Administration c. 1740-1820 (1)

6.1 A. 1740-1773

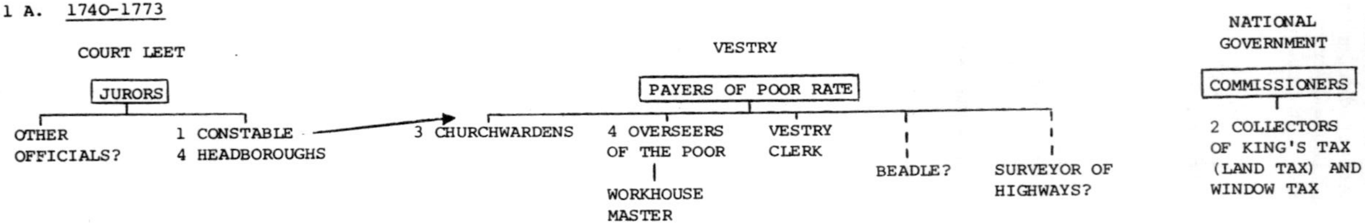

6.1 B. 1773-1810

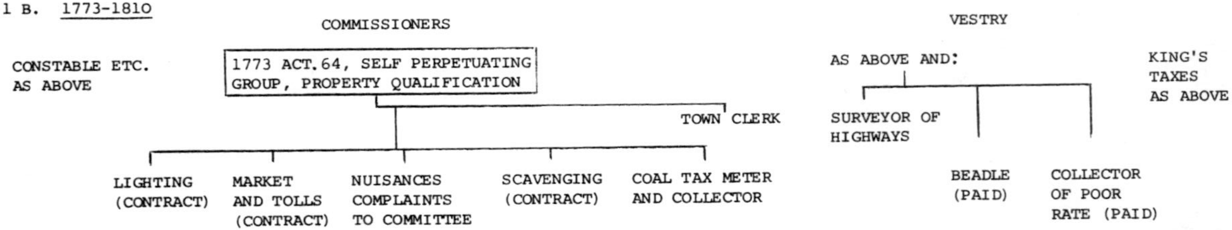

6.1 C. 1810-1820

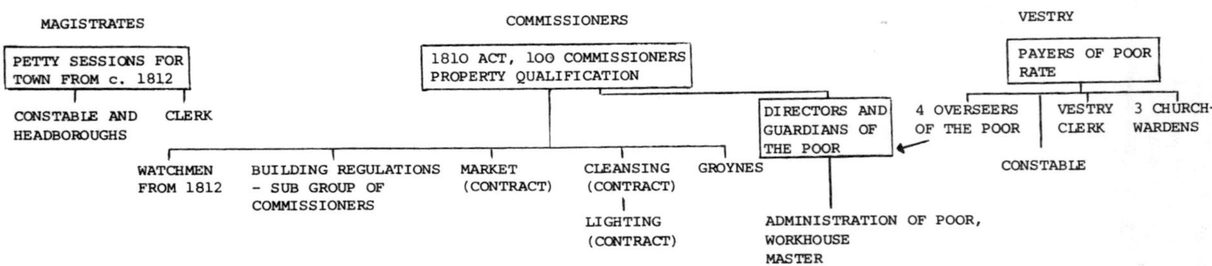

their physical or mental incapacity, could not find regular employment. Even when the workhouse was enlarged in 1800 it could only accommodate 150 which suggests that more families could afford to care for their needy without recourse to the parish.(10)

Whenever possible the overseer would ensure that the parish did not incur costs which others should bear. When applicants who wanted help were interviewed the overseers would establish whether they were residents of Brighton or if they were still chargeable to another parish. If another parish was liable for them, then the overseer would either send the applicants back to the parish of residence or, let them remain in Brighton if their own parish agreed to pay their allowances. Disputes over who should incur the cost of poor relief were resolved by the local justices who interviewed the applicants to establish their place of settlement and then made an order that committed a parish to paying. Fathers who deserted families and left them chargeable to the parish were sought and mothers of illegitimate children were asked for the names of the fathers so that the parish could order the latter to bear the cost of maintenance.(11)

Some children were apprenticed by the parish, normally to masters in the town or in the region. In 1805 some were sent to a factory in Lancashire.(12) As part of their duties the overseers arranged for innoculations of the poor and in 1784 and 1796 the population was counted in the process of organisation. (13)

When responsibility for the care of the poor passed to the Directors and Guardians of the Poor they simply replaced the vestry and the method of administration was not changed (Fig. 6). Although the sums of money collected continued to increase as the town grew in prosperity and size, the number of poor also continued to increase. One result was the building of a new workhouse just north of St. Nicholas Church (Fig. 3) which was started in 1818 and completed in 1822.(14)

The lack of an administrative body responsible for the care and regulation of the town itself until 1773 probably aggravated one of the major problems, erosion. No one was responsible for the erection and maintenance of the groynes which had been built in 1723-24 and by the late 1740s they were badly decayed. Nothing was done until 1757 when letters patent were issued which allowed the collection of house to house donations towards the cost of new groynes, estimated at £2250 which the town had been unable to raise itself. (15) Although the list of trustees for the license included men who were members of the vestry they were probably listed because they were anxious as individuals for something to be done rather than as representative of the vestry itself. It is likely that the groynes were not built, certainly erosion continued to be a problem during the early years of Brighton's development as a resort.

From the 1750s concern about erosion must have increased amongst the growing numbers of townsfolk who benefitted from the town's increasing prosperity and who were aware that land along the cliff top was increasing in value and should be protected. They may have recognised that a stable beach was an asset for seabathing, especially for bathing machines and also because ships beached in front of the town in order to deliver goods such as coal and building materials. At the same time the need to provide street cleansing and lighting and a proper market house must have been recognised. By the 1760s many English towns had town commissioners established by private acts of parliament who were responsible for the town's streets and markets. By the early 1770s townsfolk must have raised the money to pay for their act of

Parliament which was passed in 1773.

The Act's preamble is a succinct summary of the commissioners' responsibility .... 'An Act for paving, lighting, and cleansing the Streets, Lanes and Places within the town of Brighthelmstone, in the county of Sussex; for removing Nuisances and Annoyances, and preventing the like for the future; for holding and regulating a Market within the said Town; for building and repairing Groynes, in order to render the Coast safe and commodious for Ships and Vessels to unload and land Sea-Coal, Culm, and other Coal, for the Use of the Inhabitants of the said Town; and for laying a Duty thereon, and for other purposes.'(16)

Removing nuisances and annoyances included stopping butchers preparing meat in the street and coach companies having their coaches cleaned there. The commissioners were empowered by the act to collect a rate on the town to pay for administration and to fine or prosecute people who ignored their regulations.

Sixty-four commissioners were appointed by the act and they chose replacements so the body was self-perpetuating. Most of the original commissioners were important people in the town. Shergold and Hicks were leading innkeepers, Tidy owned property and Kent was a builder. Only a small group were active and they supervised the employees (Table 6.1). Most of the commissioners' responsibilities were put out to contract including scavenging (street cleaning), lighting the streets, collecting the tolls at the market, repairing and building groynes, and collecting the coal tax. The revenue from the coal tax was successfully used for the construction of groynes. The control of erosion by building and maintaining groynes improved quickly because of the revenue from the coal tax and because property developers put pressure on the commissioners. As the town spread along the cliff tops so developers agitated for the construction of more groynes and even offered to pay towards the initial cost provided the commissioners then continued to maintain them.(19)

Within the town the commissioners' activities were less successful partly because of the limited scope of the act which did not include building regulations which would empower the commissioners to insist on uncluttered street frontages free from excessively protuberant buildings or windows to help street cleansing. The contract system of cleansing caused complaints including the need to clean cesspits more frequently than the number of scavengers made possible. The town's system of street cleansing was similar to, and probably no worse than, other places but in Brighton the organisation suffered from the speed at which the town grew. The lack of sewers to drain off effluent, the slowness at which the town was paved, and the poor system of cleaning all contributed to severe pollution problems in the mid nineteenth century.

Relations between the commissioners and the ratepayers were not always amicable partly because the former did not have to subject their accounts to scrutiny by the latter and some ratepayers thought that the rapidly increasing income which the commissioners gained as the town expanded was not well spent. By the early 1800s the vestry were amongst the critics of the commissioners and wanted to make them more accountable but also to increase their powers to make them more effective. In the early 1800s there was pressure to have a police force and the town applied to parliament for a private act in order to establish one.(17)

In 1810 a new act of Parliament replaced the act of 1773. Although a hundred commissioners were listed in it of which 43 were ex-officio new commissioners were to be chosen by election from the town's ratepayers who were also to have access to the annual accounts.(18) The commissioners' powers were wider and they were permitted to appoint more paid employees (Table 6). The building regulations included provision that party walls should be nine inches thick and the power to insist that buildings which obstructed the street by being built over the building line should be re-built and correctly aligned. The commissioners became the licensing authority for the hackney carriages, bathing machines and other vehicles which plied for hire. Care of the poor was transferred from the vestry to the Directors and Guardians of the Poor which consisted of nominated commissioners (Table 6.1). Although the act empowered the commissioners to start a police force, they did not do so but a volunteer watch was organised in 1812 and some paid watchmen were employed from 1815, possibly because the town had its own petty sessions by then and the resident magistrates insisted that there should be some form of regulatory force. Not until 1821 was a proper force of watchmen organised.

Although the new commissioners had more authority than the original group because the act of 1810 was more comprehensive than the 1773 act there were still administrative problems and the standard of cleanliness of the town was considered to be unsatisfactory. During the 1810s the town's rapid growth placed severe strains upon a system of urban government which was based on unpaid amateurs. That it failed to cope effectively cannot be surprising.(19)

CONCLUSION

Between 1740 and 1820 all of the major changes in the town's physical development, economy and administration were in response to its development as a resort. The large scale projects such as Kemp Town which were built in the 1820s and 1830s around the outskirts of the Georgian resort overshadow the earlier development much of which is either in poor condition or threatened by redevelopment because it is now within the centre of the town. It is hoped that this occasional paper will contribute to a better understanding of the surviving parts of the Georgian town and encourage more interest in its history.

REFERENCES

Abbreviations

Ambulator	C. Wright, The Brighton Ambulator (1818).
B.A.L.	Brighton Area Library.
Baxter (1822);(1824)	The Stranger in Brighton and Baxter's New Brighton Directory (Brighton, 1822); Baxter's Stranger in Brighton and Directory (Brighton, 1824).
Bishop (1892)	J.G. Bishop, A Peep into the Past: Brighton in the Olden Time, People's ed. (Brighton, 1892).
B.H.	Brighton Herald.
Cobby	E. Cobby, The Brighthelmston Directory for 1800, repr. in Bishop(1892).
E.S.R.O.	East Sussex Record Office, Lewes.
Farrant (1978)	J. & S. Farrant, Aspects of Brighton 1650-1800, University of Sussex Centre for Continuing Education Occasional Paper No. 8 (1978).
Farrant (1976)	J. & S. Farrant, Brighton Before Dr. Russell, University of Sussex Centre for Continuing Education Occasional Paper No. 5 (1976).
Farrant (1980)	S. & J. Farrant, 'Brighton 1580-1820, Tudor Town to Regency Resort', Sussex Archaeological Collections, 118 (1980) forthcoming.
Ratebook 1814	B.A.L., SB352.1 B76. An Equalisation of the parish of the Houses, Stables, Coachhouses and other buildings and also of the Gardens and Inclosures in the parish of Brighthelmston. Made between April and July 1814.
S.A.S.	Sussex Archaeological Society.
S.A.C.	Sussex Archaeological Collections.
S.W.A.	Sussex Weekly Advertiser.
Topography	Attree's Topography of Brighton (Brighton 1809).

1 : THE SETTING FOR CHANGE

1 J.A.R. Pimlott, The Englishman's Holiday; A Social History (1947, repr. Hassocks, 1976), 21-48.
2 P. Borsay, 'The English Urban Renaissance: The Development of Provincial Urban Culture c. 1680-c. 1760', Social History, no. 5 (May 1977), 589-91.
3 N. Pevsner, The Buildings of England, London, V.2 (Harmondsworth,1952),23.
4 e.g. Rev. Wm. Clarke 1736: Pimlott, 52, 55.

5 Stokes, Bailey, see ref. 14 below.
6 McIntyre, see ref. 14 below.
7 Whyman (1980), Chapman, see ref. 14 below.
8 Whyman (1980), Farrant, see ref. 14 below.
9 Pimlott, 49-95, develops this point.
10 Farrant (1979), see ref. 14 below.
11 Bailey, Chapman, Temple Patterson, see ref. 14 below.
12 J. Austen, Lady Susan; The Watsons; Sanditon, ed. M. Drabble (Harmondsworth, 1974), esp. 161.
13 For a general study, see Pimlott.
14 Sources for Table 1.1. Mainly J.A. Barrett 'The Seaside Resort Towns of England and Wales', unpub. Univ. London Ph.D. (1958), 2 vols, 5,6,7,13. H.G. Stokes, The Very First History of the English Seaside (Sylvan Press), 8-106. H.K. Cook, Over the Hills and Far Away (1947), 123-129. S. McIntyre, 'Towns as Health and Pleasure Resorts; Bath, Scarborough and Weymouth, 1700-1875', unpub. Univ. Oxford D.Phil. (1973), 192, 302-3. B. Dicks, Isle of Wight (1979), 114. J. Whyman, 'A Hanoverian Watering Place, Margate before the Railway', in A. Everitt (ed.) Perspectives in English Urban History (1973), 139. J. Whyman, 'Water communications and their effect on the growth and character of Margate c. 1750-1840, unpub. paper (1980) derived from 'Aspects of holidaymaking and resort development within the Isle of Thanet with particular reference to Margate, c. 1736-c. 1840', unpub. Univ. Kent Ph.D. (1980). K.L. Mayoh, 'A Comparative Study of Resorts on the coast of Holderness', unpub. Univ. Hull M.A. (1961), 1,16,17. M.R. Oakley 'The Holiday Industry of Dorset and Somerset', unpub. Univ. Oxford B. Litt. (1964), 242. F.A. Bailey A History of Southport (Southport, 1955), 30. F. Baker, The Story of Cleethorpes and the Contribution of Methodism (Cleethorpes, 1953), 37. A. Harris, 'Seaside resorts of Westmorland and Lancashire', Trans. Hist. Soc. Lancashire and Cheshire, 115 (1963), 149. A.H. Woolner, 'The economic geography of the development and present position of Lowestoft as port and resort', unpub. London M.Sc. (econ.) (1956), 75. S. Farrant, 'Sussex by the Sea; a brief survey of the development of the seaside resorts 1730-1900', Brighton Polytechnic Geography Magazine, 6 (Dec.1979). J. Chapman, 'The Geographical evolution of Portsmouth', Portsmouth Geographical Essays (Polytechnic, 1974), 10. A. Temple Patterson A History of Southampton, (Southampton, 1966), 39.

2 : SEAFARING TOWN

1 Farrant (1978), 67-81.
2 For a more detailed account Farrant (1980).
3 Based on manorial records listed in Farrant (1978), 84-85.
4 J.G. Bishop, Brighton in 1744-61 (Brighton, 1895), 41-46, 67.
5 S. Farrant, 'The Sources and Supplies of Building Materials for Brighton c. 1770-1810', Sussex Industrial History, 10 (1980), 24. Inventories, see Farrant (1976), 19-23.
6 East Street is discussed in Farrant (1978), 44-55.
7 North Street, Farrant (1978), 56-61.
8 Bishop (1895), 58-60.
9 Farrant (1978), 81-83.
10 Bishop (1895), 46.

3 : DEVELOPMENT OF THE SEASON

1 For other texts, see Pimlott. Examples of publications which over-emphasise Russell's role abound, popular studies of the town on which more general texts base their remarks include: A. Dale, The History and

Architecture of Brighton (Brighton, 1950), and O. Sitwell and M. Barton, Brighton (1935), 46-49.
2 Whyman (1973) and paper (1980).
3 E.W. Gilbert, Brighton, Old Ocean's Bauble, (1954, repr. Hassocks, 1975), 153.
4 Sources for mortgages in Farrant (1978), 44-61.
5 Table 3.1. Population of all four towns 1801, 1811, 1821 from decennial censuses. Early figures are mostly estimates (e). Sources for Brighton: Farrant (1976), 4; Ambulator, 102. Margate: Whyman (1980). Scarborough and Weymouth: McIntyre (1973), 414, 419.
6 B. Archer, Tourist Multipliers, The State of the Art (Cardiff 1977) esp. Chap. 3. H. Robinson, Geography of Tourism (1976), 53-63.
7 Table 3.2. Brighton: 1736: J. Nichols, Literary Anecdotes of the Eighteenth Century, 2nd ed., 4 (1812), 406-407, and see Table 3.3. Margate: Whyman (1980), Scarborough and Weymouth: McIntyre (1973), 190-201, 302-314, ref. 14 in Chap. I above.
8 See Lambert's View on cover (1765), also illustrated on other topographical drawings see E.A. Hollingdale, Old Brighton (Norwich, 1979).
9 S.A.S., BRI 57, Manor Court Book.
10 Bishop (1892), 16.
11 S.W.A. 18 Feb., 3 Mar. 1760. J.A. Brent, 'The Pooles of Chailey and Lewes', Sussex Archaeological Collections 114 (1976), 75. E.S.R.O., Hook 23/1/13, building account, 1762-66.
12 Bishop (1892), 113. S.W.A., 11 Oct. 1762, 6 June 1774, 9 Nov. 1778, 21 Jan. 1793.
13 See ref. 45.
14 See ref. 45.
15 See ref. 45.
16 See ref. 45 and S.W.A. 30 Jan. 1769.
17 See ref. 45.
18 Compare the towns on Table 3.1. Overall impression from Whyman, thesis (1980).
19 S.W.A., 1759, quoted in Bishop (1892), 29.
20 See ref. 45.
21 For a description of Bath see Pimlott, 21-48. C. Lane Sayer, Correspondence of Mr. John Collier (deceased) and his Family, 2 (1907), 316, 27 July 1762, letter from Mrs. Green.
22 J. Schofield, Scarborough Guide, 2nd ed. (Hull, T. Lee, 1796) 40-46 gives a good description.
23 Furners Gardens: S.W.A., 27 June 1796; Brighton Town Hall Deeds 1604, sale to Prince of Wales.
24 S.W.A., large number of advertisements and descriptions of evening activities from the 1770s, e.g. 9 Aug. 1773, 5 July 1779, 30 June 1783.
25 S.W.A., 9 Aug. 1784, 1 Sept. 1783, 7 April 1788.
26 S.W.A., June 1758, quoted in Bishop (1892), 94-95. S.W.A., 27 July 1788, 30 Aug. 1790, 16 July 1787, 10 Aug. 1789.
27 S.W.A., 23 July 1787. Ambulator, 55.
28 Game certificates listed frequently in S.W.A. from 1787. Hunting: S.W.A. from 1769. Topography.
29 S.W.A., April 1747, quoted in Bishop (1892), 103. S.W.A., 19 March 1787, 30 July 1787, 11 Aug. 1788, 21 Jan. 1788.
30 Yachts: S.W.A., 25 July 1777. Mostly appearance of militia, S.W.A., 12 June 1780, exercises, 31 May 1790.
31 S.W.A., 26 June 1769, 5 July 1779, 5 July 1782 are some starting dates. See also Cobby (Table 3.5), Ambulator, B.H.
32 Table 3.A: 1769: Brighton Museum and Art Gallery has a 1769 Visitor's list in MS. which I will be publishing in a local journal 1980/81. S.W.A., 8 Oct. 1787. Ambulator, 102.

33 1769 list above.
34 S.W.A., quoted in Bishop (1892), 113-114. S.W.A., 16 Aug. 1779, 25 Sept. 1779, 5 Aug. 1782, Princess Amelia 19 Aug. 1782, 8 Sept. 1783 (Prince).
35 A. Relhan, A Short History of Brighthelmston (1761), ed. J.C. Michell (1892), 17.
36 Ambulator, 27.
37 Yale Univ. Lib., Thomas Turner Coll. II/17 pp. 224-5.
38 J.H. Jesse, George Selwyn and His Contemporaries, new ed. 1 (1882), 265.
39 Sayer, 2 (1907), 351: Mrs. Green, June 1763.
40 B. Cozens Hardy (ed.), The Diary of Silas Neville 1767-1788 (Cambridge, 1958), 43.
41 P.C. Yorke (ed.), The Diary of John Baker, Barrister of the Middle Temple and Solicitor General of the Leeward Islands (1931), 216-217, July 1771.
42 This is the major source of this version of the town's early history: P. Philips, A Diary Kept on An Excursion to Littlehampton near Arundel and Brighthelmstone in Sussex in 1778 and also to the latter place in 1779, 2 Vols (1780), 51.
43 For sound accounts of the town's development from 1820 see Gilbert (1954) and A. Dale, Fashionable Brighton, 2nd ed. (Newcastle, 1967).
44 Sources for Table 3.3, The Development of Resort Facilities in Georgian Brighton. Russell House: S.A.S., BRI 57, Manor Court Book. Bathing Machines, assembly rooms, coffee houses; J.J. Cartwright (ed.), The Travels Through England of Dr. Richard Pocock, 2, (1889), 104. Gardens, Library, M.C., Theatre, Chapel: Bishop (1892), 28, 40-41, 113. Housing: Manor Court Books in Farrant (1978), 48-55, 84-85. Royalty see ref. 34 in Chap. 3. Baths: S.W.A., 10 Oct. 1769, S.A.S., BRI 58, Awsiter admitted 23 Oct. 1770. Spa: A. Relhan, A short history of Brighthelmstone (1761) ed. J.C. Mitchell (1892), 45. Season: S.W.A. advertisements for Castle Inn. Visitors: S.W.A in Bishop (1892), 113-114, S.W.A., 16 Aug. 1779, 25 Sept. 1779, 5 Aug. 1772, 19 Aug. 1782. Steine: S.W.A., 23 July 1787. Races: S.W.A., 9 Aug. 1784, 1 Sept. 1783, 7 April 1788. Period 1801-20: Ambulator and Topography.

4 : THE BUILDING OF A SEASIDE RESORT

A special acknowledgement to Miss June Knight who has given so much help with the sorting and analysis of the manorial records on which this section is based.

1 Farrant (1978), 44-45. Bishop (1892), 60-61. S.W.A., 16 Aug. 1802, purchase of gardens.
2 C. Chalkin, 'Capital expenditure on buildings for cultural purposes in provincial England 1730-1830', Business History, 22 (1980), 59-60. Farrant (1978), 48, 52. Correspondence between Mr. Crunden and Samuel Shergold, in B.A.L., my thanks to Mr. D. Beevers, Keeper of Preston Manor for this reference.
3 Bishop (1892), 40. S.W.A., 22 Aug. 1774, Mr. Johnson. S.W.A., 3 Oct. 1774, fire £200 worth of clothes damaged in a chest. S.W.A., 3 Aug. 1780 completely fitted up. Chalkin (1980), 58-59.
4 S.W.A., 19 July 1790, opening. S.W.A., 5 July 1790, nearly fitted up.
5 Costs, Chalkin (1980), 59. Bishop (1892) - but his evidence is from S.W.A.
6 Farrant (1978), 44-67. J.H. and S.P. Farrant, 'Brighton 1600-1820; the antecedents and early development of a seaside resort', in P. Riden (ed.) Cardiff Papers in Local History (Dept. of Extra-Mural Studies, University College, Cardiff, forthcoming).
7 Ibid., and current research in manorial records listed in Farrant (1978), 84-86.

8 E.S.R.O., ADA 101 and 102, Manor Court Books Brighton Michelham for West Street are particularly informative. E.S.R.O., QDE/2/1/21,22,23, Land Tax.

9 Most of this information is based on current research. Some preliminary analysis in Farrant (1978), 44-67.

10 G.S. Jenks, On the Sanitary State of the Town of Brighton (1840) in B.P.P. (Lords), 1842, XXVI.

11 Compare the Ordnance Survey or street maps. Nineteenth century maps are also useful and survive for all three towns. See McIntyre for Weymouth and Scarborough.

12 C. Chalkin, The Provincial Towns of Georgian England, A Study of the building process 1740-1820 (1974), 113-39, 245-6. S. Elliott, 'The Enclosure of Stamford's Open Fields', unpub. Univ. Nottingham, M.A. (1965). Farmland: Farrant (1978), 73-81.

13 S.W.A. April 1798 issues.

14 For building materials and styles: S.P. Farrant, 'The Sources and Supplies of Building Materials for Brighton c. 1770-1810', Sussex Industrial History, 10 (1980), 23-27. Building pattern books were probably used for these houses, see list in D. Cruickshank, and P. Wyld, London: The Art of Georgian Building (1975), appendix.

15 Cliff Furlong: manorial records. T. Budgen, 'Terrier of the Laines in 1739 and 1792', copy owned by Mr. M.G. Bell, other copies in B.A.L., E.S.R.O. E.S.R.O., deposit by Hove Area Library MS 397.

16 S.W.A., 3 Oct. 1788, 30 Mar. 1789, 25 Nov. 1789, 27 June 1791, 1 April 1799, 21 Nov. 1791. E.S.R.O., Brighton Town Commissioners' Minute Books, 1800. Class and author's fieldwork.

17 W.S.R.O., Add. MS. 37, Brighton Rusper Manor Court Book. S.A.S., BRI 238, plan of area. S.A.S., BRI 59, conveyances 1782, 1785. S.W.A., 1791-1793.

18 E.S.R.O., Hove Library Deposit, 438, 941 and BRA 249. S.A.S., BRI 60, Manor Court, 1798. B.A.L., SB9 BRI Manor Court Book, 1793. S.W.A., 26 Aug. 1799. Topography 18-19. Rate Book 1814. Baxter (1822). Dale (1967), 38-39.

19 Rate Book 1814. Fig. 5 Cobby's map 1800. Fig. 6 Marchant 1808.

20 1792 Terrier (ref. 15 above). S.W.A., 18 July 1788, 30 Mar. 1789, 20 Feb. 1797, 16 Feb. 1798. B.H., 6 June 1807, 27 June 1807, 7 Mar. 1807, 6 Sept. 1806. S.A.S., N 596, N 589, N 728-39, N 825. Cobby. Rate Book 1814. Baxter (1822),(1824). Manor Court Books: S.A.S., BRI 24-25, BRI 59-61; B.A.L., SB9 BRI.

21 Jenks (1842). Brighton Town Hall (Secretary's Dept.) copy of night-watch's record book 1822.

22 Hilly Laine: Terrier 1792, S.W.A., 9 April 1798, 9 April 1799, 7 June 1800, Feb. 1805, 10 June 1805. B.H., 18 April 1807, June 1807, 15 Nov. 1806, 26 Sept. 1807. Preston Manor EX/A/38. S.A.S. E162. B.A.L., SB 346,B 76 Act 40 Geo 111 1800, C.S. Dickens. 1814 Rate Book. Cobby. Baxter (1822), (1824). E.S.R.O., Hove Library BRA 1544 Waterloo Place. Manor Court Books.

23 North Laine: S.W.A., 28 July 1788, Mar., May, Oct., Dec., 1789, 12 April 1790, 19 May 1790, 19 Jan. 1795, 21 April 1800, 14 May 1804. B.H., 20 June 1807, 5 Sept. 1807, Brighton Ratebook 1814. Baxter (1822), (1824). Topography. Cobby. Manor Court Books.

24 West Laine: E.S.R.O., Hove Library deposit 29/40, 405, 595, 657, 645, 862. BRA 387. S.A.S., N 576, N 708, 674-75. S.A.S., BRI 2-6. S.A.S., B 71, 73-74. S.W.A., 26 Nov. 1792, 14 Jan. 1793, April 1800, 1 Sept. 1800, 16 Aug. 1802, 18 Jan. 1805, 28 Oct. 1805, 29 Aug. 1807, 4 July 1807. B.H., 22 Nov. 1806, 15 Nov. 1806, 20 Dec. 1806, 6 Dec. 1806, 11 April 1807, 28 Nov. 1807, 17 Oct. 1807. Directories and Manor Court Books as above.

25 Decennial Census.
26 Baxter (1822), (1824).
27 Dale (1967), for a good study of Brighton's architecture.

5 : POPULATION AND EMPLOYMENT

1 C.M. Law, 'Some notes on the urban population of England and Wales in the Eighteenth Century', Local Historian, 10 (1972). J. Huzel, 'Population Change in an East Sussex Town: Lewes 1660-1800, Sussex Industrial History, 3 (Winter 1971/72), 2-4.
2 Farrant (1978), 16-24.
3 S.W.A.: based mainly upon abstraction of all references to businesses, done by Mr. R.G. Martin.
4 Cobby, Baxter (1822), (1824) sector analysis is by author.
5 Baxter (1824). P. Wilde, 'The use of business directories in comparing the industrial structures of towns', Local Historian, 12 (1976) 152-156. E.P. Duggan, 'Industrialisation and the development of urban business communities: research problems, sources and techniques', Local Historian, 11 (1975), 457-465.
6 Analysis by occupational sector based on work by Mrs. J. Lank.
7 Analysis of Baxter (1822) and (1824) based on work by Mrs. J. Lank and Miss S. Preece. Limitations of sources G. Shaw 'The content and reliability of 19th century trade directories', Local Historian, 13 (1978).
8 P. Barfoot and J. Wilkes, The Universal British Directory, 2 (1793). S.W.A. advertisements. Cobby.
9 Baxter (1822), 1824).
10 Population, table 3.2.
11 Baileys British Directory (1784) 4, Barfoot and Wilkes. Cobby. Baxter (1822), (1824).

6 : ADMINISTRATION

1 Table 6 and paragraph based on sources below. Bishop (1895) reproduces extracts from the poor rate book and listed the parish officers, 1744-1761. A. Dale, Brighton Town and Brighton People (Chichester, 1976) is mainly extracts and notes from the Commissioners' Minutes and vestry minute books from c. 1779 but does not examine which commissioners were active or the finances. The original minute books which have been used for this paper are now in E.S.R.O. and would repay more detailed analysis than Dale applied.
2 B.A.L., SB 343 M 27, Magistrates' Clerk's Books, 8 April 1816, J.P.s still confirming appointment of constable and headboroughs.
3 Bishop (1895), 12. S.W.A. 6 May 1771. References to excise officers' activities in S.W.A. esp. Jan./Feb. 1777, Sept. 1783 - Feb. 1784.
4 F. Vigier, Change and Apathy, Liverpool and Manchester during the Industrial Revolution (Cambridge, Mass., 1970), 105-110.
5 Bishop (1895), 76, table.
6 See Dale (1976), sections on Vestry. Notices placed in S.W.A.
7 Bishop (1895) 76, table recalculated.
8 Bishop (1895) 12, 41-46.
9 Farrant (1980).
10 Bishop (1895), 60. S.W.A., 16 Feb. 1785 nets - typical advertisement. E.S.R.O., Brighton Vestry Book 13 Jan. 1790. S.W.A., 7 Dec. 1789. Dale (1976) enlarged 1800, 9; 1818, 37.
11 S.W.A., 9 May 1791, 2 Jan. 1797. Bishop (1895) 61, M.J. Burchall (ed.), Eastern Sussex Settlement Certificates (Brighton: Sussex Genealogical Centre,1979), i-ii.
12 A. Dale (1976) 13.

13 Dunvan see Section 1.1.

14 See 10.

15 A. Relhan (1761), 13, 64. Farrant (1980).

16 B.A.L., SB 346, Act 13 Geo III c xxxiv 1773.

17 E.S.R.O. Commissioner's Minutes 1800-1801 contains examples of negotiations about groynes. Other responsibilities evident in minutes and from newspapers e.g. contracts, tolls: S.W.A. 15 Mar. 1790, 24 June 1790, 6 Jan. 1792, 17 April 1797. B.H., 24 June 1813 in B.A.L., 34593, newspaper cuttings. Dale (1976) does discuss this but chronological structure of book limits scope. B.H., 28 Feb. 1807, 7 Mar. 1807, 11 April 1807.

18 Dale (1976) section on 1810-20. Magistrates Books op. cit.

19 Dale (1976). Copies of all the Acts are in B.A.L.

SOURCES FOR THE FIGURES

Cover. J. Lambert. Brighthelmston from the east, 1765. Reproduced from print owned by Mr. K.T.N. Bryant. Brighton Museum and Art Gallery owns a copy and see Gilbert, Plate I.

Fig. 1. E.S.R.O., AMS4106 and B.A.L. SB 9 BRI (acc. no. 74318), map and book of reference giving the ownership of the laines on 1792 and, in the book, in 1738/9. The sheepdown ploughed up between the two dates is shown as down. The groynes in the front of the town are from C. Lempriere, 'South view of Brighton in the year 1743' (Sketch in Brighton Museum and Art Gallery).

Fig. 2. Outline based upon Fig. 3 but it is only intended to show where buildings stood and would not have been as densely built up as the stippled area suggests. Key based on 1744 rate book and on manor court book entries.

Fig. 3. Yeakell and Gardner's survey of Brighthelmston, 1779. This is reproduced more frequently than Fig. 4 below. The 'infilling' is only generalised, this map is less accurate than Fig. 4.

Fig. 4. T. Budgen, A new and correct plan of Brighthelmstone (Brighton, Sept. 1788). The only known original copy is British Library, K.42.16.

Fig. 5. Map of Brighthelmston in Cobby, reproduced on J.G. Bishop, Brighton in the Olden Time (1880) 1. From Mr. K.T.N. Bryant.

Fig. 6. J. Marchant, Brighthelmstone (1 Sept. 1808). Reproduced in Topography.

Fig. 7. 'Brighthelmston, 1822', map in Baxter (1822).